CONTENTS

First published by Ebury Press 1965
Reprinted 1968
Revised edition 1970
Reprinted 1971, 1972, 1973, 1974
Revised edition 1976

© The National Magazine Co. Ltd 1965

ISBN 0 85223 101 6

Photographs by Kenneth Swain and Anthony Kay
Cover design by John Gordon

Printed in Great Britain by BAS Printers Limited
Wallop, Hampshire
and bound by Hazell Watson & Viney Ltd
Aylesbury, Bucks

GOOD HOUSEKEEPING
COOKING IS FUN

Compiled by **Good Housekeeping Institute**

EBURY PRESS · London

FOREWORD

This is the third edition of Good Housekeeping's established school favourite *Cooking is Fun*. Once more we have brought it up to date by including some new recipes showing new methods and ideas. To make the book even easier to use, the sections have been colour coded. You can now see at a glance where each chapter begins—for example, the lunch time recipes come in the yellow and pink sections, while the blue section is supper recipes. Short introductions have been added to each chapter to help with planning meals.

CAROL MACARTNEY
Director,
Good Housekeeping Institute

INTRODUCTION

Of all teachers, those dealing with home economics must be most aware of changes in the contemporary scene. We cannot put the clock back, but must be prepared to accept changes in family life and ways of living. Advances in food technology and today's greater understanding of nutritional problems must both influence what we teach those pupils who, in such a short time, will be the next generation of working homemakers.

Therefore, it gives me in my private capacity great pleasure to write a foreword to this book. Its attractive production, lavish use of photographs and up-to-date approach to cookery fully justify its title, "Cooking is Fun". The older pupil will be encouraged to use the book independently and with confidence.

Teachers will recognise that this book has been planned with real understanding of modern educational thought in home economics. It is not only a recipe book—sound nutritional values are implicit throughout its pages. Its emphasis on complete meals—as opposed to individual dishes—the inclusion of simple theory work and the intelligent use of "convenience" foods should all prove most valuable. The help it gives in planning and organising meals of different types, with emphasis on speed and method, will prepare schoolchildren for a twentieth-century future.

Many teachers have to consider preparation for the examination of the Certificate of Secondary Education. This book, with its careful cross-references and really adequate index, should prove most useful to teacher and pupil; speaking personally I thoroughly recommend it.

BRENDA C. FRANCIS
Inspector of Home Economics for the
Inner London Education Authority

BEFORE YOU START WORK . . .

1 Put on an apron

2 Always wash your hands

3 Read the recipe all through before beginning—and see note below

4 Collect up all the utensils

5 Find all the ingredients

6 Remember that it's important to weigh or measure all the quantities exactly

7 Be sure to follow the recipe step by step

IMPORTANT

Except in the case of Cakes, Bread, etc., all recipes in this book give 4 average servings, unless otherwise stated.

NOTE

Abbreviations used in this book are as follows:

kg = **kilo(gram(s))**	**tsp(s).** = **teaspoon(s)**
g = **gram(s)**	**tbsp(s).** = **tablespoon(s)**
ml = **millilitre(s)**	**in.** = **inch(es)**
cm = **centimetre(s)**	**min(s).** = **minute(s)**
mm = **millimetre(s)**	

COOKING

Peeling

Scraping

Shredding

Slicing

6

TERMS

Chipping

Dicing

Chopping an Onion

Chopping Parsley

7

Draining

Straining

Sieving

Grating

8

Levelling a
tablespoonful

Measuring half
a tablespoonful

Measuring a
quarter tablespoonful

Rubbing in

Creaming

Folding in

Dropping
consistency

Beating

Whisking

Blending

Kneading

Glazing

PEELING TOMATOES

Half-fill a pan with water, bring to the boil and remove from
the heat. Put the tomatoes in, using a spoon so as not to
splash yourself with the hot water. Count up to 5. Remove
the tomatoes, again using the spoon, and plunge them into
a bowl half-filled with cold water. Take the tomatoes out one
by one and carefully peel off the loosened skins, using a
vegetable knife.

(See picture A)

MAKING STOCK WITH A BOUILLON CUBE

Put a kettle on to boil. Crumble a bouillon cube into a
measuring jug, then pour on 375 ml boiling water. Stir once
or twice to mix well.

(See picture B)

A   B

METHODS

SEASONED FLOUR

Put some flour on a plate, sprinkle generously with salt and pepper and mix well. Use to coat meat, etc., before frying or stewing.

(See picture C)

DEEP FAT FRYING

You need a strong pan which is at least 10–13 cm deep. Half-fill it with fat and heat slowly; when you think it is hot enough, test as follows with a small cube of crustless bread. If the bread becomes golden-brown in 60–70 seconds, the fat is hot enough for uncooked foods such as apple fritters. If it browns in 40–50 seconds, it is right for cooked mixtures such as rissoles.

Lower the food to be fried slowly into the pan, or the fat will rise over the edge of the pan. Don't put in too much food at a time or it will lower the temperature of the fat and will not cook properly. Drain the cooked food on absorbent kitchen paper (crumple it up a little first).

(See picture D)

C

D

SEPARATING EGGS

You will need 3 basins—one to work over, one to hold all the egg whites and one for the yolks. Holding the egg over the first basin, use a knife to crack the shell in half. Pull the two halves apart, taking great care to keep the unbroken yolk in one half of the shell. Pour the white that is left in the second half-shell into the basin. Now transfer the yolk carefully to the second half, letting all the remaining white drop into the basin. It is very important not to break the yolk. Put the yolk into the second basin and the white into the third. Crack the remaining eggs one by one into the first basin, so that if any yolk breaks, the rest of the eggs are not spoilt.

(*See picture A*)

ROLLING OUT PASTRY

Roll it out on a floured board, using light but firm strokes. Always roll away from yourself, never sideways, as this gives an uneven pastry.

When moving the pastry, take great care not to stretch it, or it will shrink during cooking and go out of shape. If you are rolling the pastry to a round shape, turn it round a little after each forward-and-back stroke—always turning it in the same direction.

(*See picture B*)

A

B

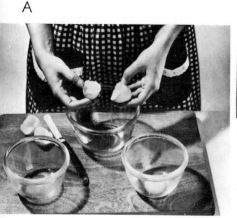

LINING A ROUND CAKE TIN

Stand the tin on the corner of a sheet of greaseproof paper and draw round it, using a pencil. Cut out the round of paper just inside the pencil line. Measure the depth of the tin, add on an extra 5 cm and cut a strip of greaseproof paper this width. (It may be necessary to cut two pieces to give a strip long enough to go right round the tin.) Turn up 1 cm along one long edge of the strip and make slanting cuts at 1 cm intervals. Grease the inside of the tin and fit the strips into place round the edge, with the snipped edge on the base, to give a neat lining. Fit the round of paper into the bottom. Grease all the lining paper thoroughly.

(See picture C)

LINING AN OBLONG TIN

Cut a piece of paper about 5 cm larger all round than the tin. Place the tin on it and at each corner make a cut from the angle of the paper to the corner of the tin. Grease the inside of the tin, put in the paper so that it fits closely, overlapping at the corners, then grease the lining well.

(See picture D)

C D

TO COVER A PUDDING FOR STEAMING

Pleat a square of greased greaseproof paper and place over the pudding to allow for rising.

Cover with a clean cloth tied round the rim of the basin and knot the ends over the top of the pudding.

Alternatively cover with aluminium foil and tie or twist it under the rim of the basin.

TO BLANCH ALMONDS

Place almonds in a small saucepan and pour over sufficient boiling water to cover. Allow to stand for a few minutes. Drain the almonds and slide off the skins.

TO SPLIT ALMONDS

Place almonds between thumb and finger. Insert a sharp knife at the pointed end of the almonds to separate the two halves.

This meal must be quick and easy to prepare, yet satisfying enough to keep you going until lunch-time. For many people the favourite menu is: Fruit, fruit juice and a cereal, followed by toast, butter and marmalade, with tea or coffee to drink (see page 198).

1 If possible, lay the table the evening before and get out all the utensils you will need for the breakfast, to save time in the morning. Prepare the fruit, if necessary (see below).

2 Most people like a drink as soon as possible, so first of all put on the kettle, then light the grill for the toast.

3 These are some of the most popular items for the fruit course:

Grapefruit: Cut the grapefruit in half. Using a sharp-pointed knife, cut all the way round each half between the skin and the flesh, then cut between the segments, so that each piece can be lifted out easily. Remove the core. Sprinkle the fruit with sugar and put into individual dishes.

Stewed Fruit: Any stewed fruit that has been cooked beforehand and kept in a cool place is suitable—for instance, apples, plums, rhubarb. Sometimes some stewed fruit is left over when a pie is made.

Dried Fruit: e.g., prunes, figs. These also are prepared beforehand and kept in a cool place. Wash the fruit well and soak it for some hours or overnight in just enough water to cover, then put into a saucepan with 50 g sugar for every 200 g fruit, bring to the boil and simmer gently until tender. Remove the fruit, boil the juice for a few minutes, until syrupy, then pour it over the fruit.

Fruit Juice: Canned juice is easiest to use, so keep a can in the store cupboard. If you have fruit juice regularly, buy a large can, pour the contents into a jug and keep it in the refrigerator, using a little each day. Remember to put another can in the refrigerator a day before the first is finished, so that it is already chilled when you open it.

4 *Cereals:* The packet kinds are very popular and there are very many sorts to ring the changes. Serve hot or cold milk with them; some are sweetened, but don't forget to put sugar on the table for the unsweetened kinds. Dress up cereals sometimes by adding something different—brown sugar or syrup, a sliced banana or a little stewed fruit.

Porridge is enjoyed by many people and the quick types now available are easily made. Porridge makes you feel warm inside before going out on a cold winter's morning! On holiday, try something special, such as Muesli, which is a Swiss breakfast dish. Mix 50 g sultanas or raisins with 4 tbsps. rolled oats and add 125 ml milk. Allow to stand for a little while (overnight if possible), then grate 2–3 eating apples into the mixture and add 1 tbsp. brown sugar or honey and a few chopped nuts. Mix well and serve at once. Any other fruit can be added—sliced orange, halved grapes or sliced banana.

5 *Toast:* The best kind is made by using fairly thick slices of bread and toasting them under a hot grill until evenly browned—watch them carefully! Don't pile the slices one upon the other or the toast will go soggy; if possible, use a toast rack, as it holds the slices on edge so that the steam can escape. Make toast just before serving, as it becomes hard if it is kept some time. Serve with butter and marmalade.

6 Make the tea or coffee.

A COOKED BREAKFAST

Even people who take only a light breakfast during the week often enjoy a cooked one at weekends, when there may be more time to spare in the morning. First of all put the plates to warm, then cook the food—for instance, one of the dishes described below:

FRIED EGGS

Ingredients	Utensils
50 g lard	Frying pan
4 eggs	Cup
	Tablespoon
	Palette knife or slice
	Plate

1 Melt 15 g lard in the frying pan.

2 Break an egg into the cup, then slide the egg carefully into the hot fat, tipping the frying pan so that the egg does not spread too far. Use the tablespoon to pour the hot fat over it, so that it cooks evenly both on top and underneath.

3 When the egg is just set, remove it from the pan, using the palette knife or slice, and put it onto a hot plate to keep warm.

4 Cook the other eggs in the same way, adding fat as necessary.

GRILLED BACON

Ingredients	Utensils
4 rashers of bacon	Kitchen scissors, tablespoon, fork
	Grillpan and rack

1 Heat the grill to a moderate heat.

2 Cut the rind from the bacon, using the scissors; you can also snip the bacon fat at intervals, to stop the rashers curling during the cooking.

3 Put the rashers side by side on the rack in the grillpan, then put the pan under the grill.

4 After a few minutes, when the bacon fat has changed colour, remove the grillpan from the heat and use a spoon and fork to turn the rashers over. Replace the pan under the grill and cook the other side of the bacon.

5 Grill the bacon until it is cooked to your liking. Serve as soon as possible.

GRILLED TOMATOES

Ingredients	Utensils
4 tomatoes	Fork, knife, tablespoon
Salt and pepper	Grillpan and rack
A knob of butter	

1 Heat the grill to a moderate heat.

2 Cut the tomatoes in half, sprinkle with salt and pepper, then put a small piece of butter on each half.

3 Place the tomatoes on the rack in the grillpan and put under the grill.

4 Cook for 5 minutes.

LUNCH

This meal is generally the lighter of the two main meals that should be eaten throughout the day and will vary considerably depending on the ages and activities of the family. It usually consists of a main course followed by either a sweet course or cheese and biscuits. A light dish such as soup or hors d'oeuvres can be served before the main course.

To ensure that the meal is appetising and nutritious there are certain points to remember:

1 The meal should contain a protein dish, for example, meat, fish, eggs or cheese. This dish can be hot or cold depending on the time of year and the amount of time available to prepare it.

2 Vegetables are an important part of the meal and may be served separately or as the basis of the main course in dishes such as Cauliflower Cheese. A salad may be served instead of vegetables either as an additional dish or as part of the main course.

3 The sweet course usually takes the form of something light such as stewed fruit or fresh fruit. If you serve cheese and biscuits instead, include something crisp such as celery or watercress.

4 When choosing dishes to make up the meal remember that colour and texture are most important. Select dishes that will give a contrast of flavour, texture and colour.

CASEROLED BEEF AND TOMATOES

Ingredients	Utensils
700 g chuck steak	Cook's knife, tablespoon,
Salt and pepper	wooden spoon, vegetable
1 onion	knife
50 g lard or dripping	Chopping board
2 level tbsps. flour	2 large saucepans
250 ml bouillon cube stock	Ovenproof casserole
1 tbsp. Worcestershire	Measuring jug
sauce (if available)	Large bowl
400 g tomatoes	
2 sticks of celery (if	
available)	

1 Heat the oven to 180°C. (350°F.), mark 4.

2 Cut the meat into 3 cm cubes, using the cook's knife, and sprinkle with salt and pepper.

3 Peel and slice the onion. Melt the fat in a saucepan, add the onion and fry until soft. Remove the onion, draining well (see picture A), and put in the casserole. Add the meat to the fat, fry until brown, remove, draining well, and add to the onions.

4 Sprinkle the flour into the pan, mix with the fat, using the wooden spoon, and fry until brown (see picture B). Add the stock and Worcestershire sauce and bring to the boil, stirring all the time.

5 Bring a pan of water to the boil, put in the tomatoes and count up to 5; remove the tomatoes and plunge them into a bowl of cold water. The skins can now be easily peeled off with a vegetable knife. Cut each tomato into four.

6 Cut the celery into pieces 1 cm long.

7 Add tomatoes and celery to the mixture in the pan.

8 Transfer the mixture to the casserole and cook in the oven for 1½ hours. If preferred, continue cooking on top of the stove in the pan on a very low heat.

Serve boiled potatoes and a green vegetable with your casserole and follow it by something fairly firm, such as Egg Custard Tart.

For casseroles, stews and braising choose cheaper cuts of meat, such as flank, chuck, brisket.

For roasting or grilling choose prime cuts—rib, sirloin, topside.

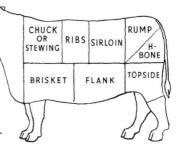

A

B

RAGOÛT OF LIVER

Ingredients
450 g calf's liver
4 level tbsps. flour
Salt and pepper
4 rashers of bacon
1 cooking apple
25 g margarine
375 g bouillon cube
  stock
100 g rice
25 g cleaned sultanas
1 tsp. tomato paste

Utensils
Bowl
Cook's knife, vegetable
  knife, tablespoon, teaspoon
Plate
Frying pan
Measuring jug
Wooden spoon
Serving dish

1 Wash the liver in cold water and cut it into small pieces, removing any skin or tubes (see picture A).

2 Measure the flour onto the plate and season well with salt and pepper. Dip the pieces of liver in this seasoned flour (picture B).

3 Cut the rind from the bacon and cut each rasher into 8 pieces (picture C).

4 Peel the apple and cut into quarters. Remove the core, then cut the apple quarters into cubes (picture D).

5 Melt the fat in the pan and fry the liver and bacon until golden-brown.

6 Add the stock, stirring all the time with the wooden spoon to prevent the sauce burning.

7 Add the rice, sultanas, apple and tomato paste.

8 Simmer for 20 minutes, or until the rice is cooked. Pour into a deep serving dish.

Serve with mashed potatoes and sliced carrots, then have something exciting like Apple Amber.

Ox liver is the cheapest type, but as its flavour is strong and the flesh is usually coarse in texture, it is generally used for casseroles, stews and so on.

Calf's liver is regarded as the best type for frying or grilling and is rather expensive. Lamb's liver also can be fried or grilled, but must be cooked gently to prevent it becoming tough.

Pig's liver has a very strong flavour and some people do not like it.

SAVOURY LAMB CHOPS

Ingredients	Utensils
4 lamb chops	Cook's knife, vegetable
2 onions	knife, tablespoon
3 tomatoes	Chopping board
100 g mushrooms	Small saucepan
Salt and pepper	Small bowl
Margarine	Ovenproof casserole

1 Heat the oven to 200°C. (400°F.), mark 6.

2 Trim any unwanted fat from the chops.

3 Peel and slice the onions.

4 Boil a pan of water, put in tomatoes and count up to 5; transfer tomatoes to a bowl of cold water—the skins can now be peeled off with a knife. Slice tomatoes (picture A).

5 Wash and slice the mushrooms.

6 Place the onions, tomatoes and mushrooms in the casserole (picture B) and arrange the chops on top.

7 Put salt, pepper and a knob of margarine on each chop.

8 Cover and cook near the bottom of the oven for 1 hour.

Bake jacket potatoes in the oven with the chops and serve cabbage as a second vegetable. Syrup layer pudding could finish a substantial meal.

Lamb is taken from a sheep one year old—after that age the meat is known as mutton and is generally stronger-flavoured —and cheaper—than lamb.

For roasting, choose leg, shoulder and loin.
Loin, chump and best end are good for frying and grilling.
Use breast, scrag or neck for cheap stews; best end makes a really delicious stew or casserole.

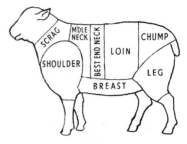

You will find in the shops a lot of good quality lamb from England, Wales and Scotland, as well as the imported New Zealand meat, which is also known as Canterbury lamb.

SMOTHERED CHOPS

Put some lamb chops in a dish (allowing at least 1 per person) and top with a thinly sliced lemon (leave the rind on). Add 2 onions and 1 green pepper, both thinly sliced; pour some canned tomatoes round the chops and cook as for Savoury Chops. Sprinkle with chopped parsley.

A

B

PORK AND PINEAPPLE

Ingredients	Utensils
4 pork chops	A fireproof serving dish
Salt and pepper	Can opener
A medium-sized can of	Sieve
pineapple rings	Basin
1 tbsp. lemon juice	Knife, tablespoon
25 g brown sugar	

1 Heat the oven to 180°C. (350°F.), mark 4.

2 Trim any unwanted fat from the meat. Wash the chops and arrange in the serving dish.

3 Sprinkle the chops with salt and pepper.

4 Open the can of pineapple rings.

5 Drain off the juice by tipping the contents of the can into a sieve over a basin (picture A).

6 Pour the juice over the chops in the dish. Add 1 tbsp. lemon juice. Put the dish in the oven.

7 After 45 minutes take the dish from the oven. Alter the oven to 220°C. (425°F.), mark 7.

8 Place a pineapple ring on each chop and sprinkle with sugar (picture B). Put back in the oven for 10 minutes.

Where does a chop come from?

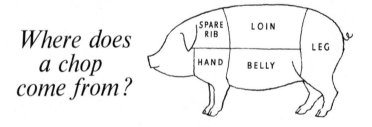

How much does this dish cost?

What vegetables could you serve with it?

Which pudding would you like to follow it?

PORK CHOPS

Chops can be grilled to make a meal in a hurry. First heat the grill, cook the chops for 10 minutes, turn them carefully and cook for a further 10 minutes on the other side. Make a quick sauce like this: remove chops and grill rack, pour off any surplus fat, put the chops back in the bottom of the grillpan and pour in 125 ml cider, stirring with a wooden spoon to mix in all the meat juices. Heat gently and serve the chops with the sauce poured over them.

Creamed or new potatoes and French beans could be served with the chops; to follow, you could have Baked Jam Roll.

A   B

SPANISH SAUSAGES

Ingredients	Utensils
1 onion	Chopping board, vegetable
1 green pepper (if liked)	knife
50 g margarine	Frying pan
450 g sausages	Teaspoon, tablespoon,
2 level tsps. salt	wooden spoon
1 bay leaf and 2 cloves	Basin
A medium-sized can of	Serving dish
tomatoes	
1 level tsp. sugar	
3 tbsps. plain flour	
6 tbsps. water	

1 Peel the onion and cut it into slices. Chop the pepper, discarding the seeds and stem.

2 Melt the fat in the frying pan. Add all the ingredients except the flour and water, cover and simmer for 30 minutes.

3 Mix the flour and water to a smooth paste in the basin. Add some of the hot liquid from the pan to this and mix well with the wooden spoon.

4 Pour the flour mixture into the pan and simmer gently, stirring all the time, until the sauce thickens.

5 Remove the bay leaf and cloves before serving. Serve with creamed potatoes.

Bake an Apple Charlotte in the oven at the same time.

Sausages are a very handy stand-by, as they can be cooked in many different ways. Remember that chipolata sausages cook more quickly than thick ones.

Some people prick sausages so that they do not burst when being cooked, but others prefer not to as they think it spoils their appearance. Which do you think is the better way?

Always store sausages of any type in as cool a place as possible.

Frying Sausages: Melt a little fat in the frying pan, add the sausages and fry over a gentle heat (to prevent their burning), for 15–20 minutes. Serve with mashed potato—see picture.

Grilling Sausages: This is perhaps the most popular method. Heat the grill to hot, put the sausages on the grill rack in the pan and cook until one side is lightly browned, then turn them; continue cooking and turning them frequently for about 15–20 minutes, when the sausages will be well browned.

Baking Sausages: This is the easiest way. Heat the oven to 200°C. (400°F.), mark 6. Put the sausages in a greased baking tin and cook in the centre of the oven for 30 minutes.

A tasty way with sausage-meat is to make it into Sausage Cakes. Mix 450 g sausage-meat with 1 grated onion and 1 tsp. mixed dried herbs. Divide the mixture into 8 and shape each portion into a round cake. Heat 25 g fat in a frying pan and fry the cakes over a low heat for 10 minutes; turn them and fry the other side until crisp and brown.

STEAK AND KIDNEY PUDDING

Ingredients

For the Filling
450 g stewing steak
1 sheep's kidney
2 level tbsps. flour
Salt and pepper
1 onion
Stock
For the Pastry
200 g self-raising flour
1 level tsp. salt
100 g suet
125 ml water

Utensils

Steamer or large pan
1½-pint pudding basin
Greaseproof paper, string
Sharp cook's knife,
 round-bladed knife,
 tablespoon, teaspoon
Chopping board
Plate
Sieve, mixing bowl
Measuring jug
Pastry board, dredger,
 rolling pin, pastry brush

1 Boil some water in the steamer or saucepan.

2 Cut out a double piece of greaseproof paper 5–8 cm larger all round than the top of the basin. Grease the centre of the paper and the inside of the basin.

3 Cut the meat and kidney up small, trimming off any fat, skin or gristle. Put the flour on a plate and add salt and pepper; roll the meat in this. Peel and chop the onion.

4 *Make Suetcrust Pastry:* Sift the flour and salt into the bowl; stir in the suet with a round-bladed knife and add nearly all the water, to make a soft, elastic dough.

5 Turn the pastry on to a floured board, knead lightly and roll into a round 5 cm larger than basin. Cut out one quarter of the round and keep for a lid (picture A).

6 Put the rest of the pastry into the basin, pressing it against the sides but without stretching it; overlap the cut edges, damp them and press firmly together (picture B).

7 Form the remaining quarter of pastry into a round and roll out to fit the top of the basin (picture C).

8 Fill basin with layers of meat and onion, add 4 tbsps. stock, damp top edge of pastry, press on "lid" (picture D).

9 Cover the basin with paper and tie on. Place in steamer or saucepan and steam for $3\frac{1}{2}$–4 hours. If necessary, top up the water, which must not be allowed to boil away.

Note: If the meat is first stewed for $\frac{1}{2}$ hour, the cooking time can be reduced to 3 hours.

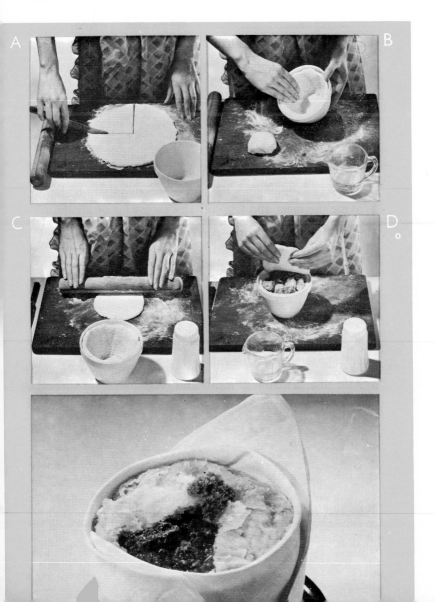

HOT-POT

Ingredients

450 g shoulder beefsteak
   or best end of neck of
   mutton
50 g flour
Salt and pepper
2 onions, 2 carrots
2–3 sticks of celery
   (optional)
600 g potatoes
375 ml bouillon cube stock
25 g margarine

Utensils

A deep casserole
Chopping board
Cook's knife, vegetable
   knife, potato peeler,
   tablespoon
Measuring jug
Pastry brush

1 Heat the oven to 325°F. (163°C.), mark 3. Grease the casserole.

2 Wipe the meat and trim off any excess fat or gristle.

3 Cut the meat into even-sized pieces or chops (picture A). Mix the flour with a little salt and pepper on a plate and toss the meat in this seasoned flour.

4 Peel the onions and slice them into rings. Wash and chop the celery. Peel the carrots and slice into rounds. Peel the potatoes and slice them fairly thickly (picture B).

5 Put half the meat into the deep casserole, cover with a layer of vegetables and sprinkle with salt and pepper.

6 Add the remaining meat and vegetables (picture C), ending with potato (picture D) and sprinkling with seasoning.

7 Add the stock to the casserole and cover with a lid or aluminium foil.

8 Bake in the centre of the oven for about 2 hours. Uncover the dish, brush the top of the potatoes with the melted fat and bake uncovered for a final $\frac{1}{2}$ hour, until the potatoes are crisp and brown.

Hot-pot is complete in itself and does not really need any other vegetables as accompaniment. It's a good dish to cook when you have a busy day, as it can safely be left in the oven while you are shopping or doing other work in the house.

Do you think it is a cheap or expensive dish?

What would you like after it—jam tart or a steamed pudding?

BAKED STUFFED LIVER

Ingredients	Utensils
450 g pig's liver	Shallow casserole or
2 thick slices of white	ovenproof dish
bread (100 g)	Kitchen scissors, cook's
1 small onion	knife, teaspoon, fork
1 tsp. mixed herbs	Chopping board
Salt and pepper	Grater, plate
25 g margarine	2 basins
1 egg or milk to mix	Saucepan
100 g streaky bacon	Measuring jug
250 ml bouillon cube	
stock	

1 Heat the oven to 180°C. (350°F.), mark 4. Grease the casserole.

2 Wash the liver and trim off any tubes or skin. Cut into 8 pieces and place these side by side in the casserole.

3 Holding the grater on a plate, rub the bread against the rough side until it forms breadcrumbs.

4 Peel, then chop or grate the onion, put it into a basin and mix with the breadcrumbs, herbs, salt and pepper.

5 Melt the margarine in a saucepan. Whisk the egg in a basin with a fork. Add the melted fat and enough of the egg (or milk) to the crumb mixture to make it stick together.

6 Spread some of this stuffing on top of the liver, pressing it well down (picture A).

7 Rind the bacon, cut it into 8 pieces and arrange over the stuffing (picture B).

8 Pour the stock round the liver. Cover the dish with a lid, greaseproof paper or aluminium foil and bake in the centre of the oven for about 20 minutes. The lid may then be removed for the last 10 minutes of the cooking time, to crisp the bacon.

A stuffing is a good way of adding extra flavour to a dish and will make it more filling without being expensive. This herb stuffing can also be spread on chops, which are then baked.

If you want to make a still more interesting stuffing, try this one: Mix together in a basin 50 g chopped suet, 50 g chopped bacon, 100 g fresh breadcrumbs, 1 tbsp. chopped parsley, $\frac{1}{2}$ tsp. mixed herbs, the grated rind of $\frac{1}{2}$ a lemon and some salt and pepper; beat an egg in a basin and gradually add to dry ingredients until mixture sticks together.

Serve Stuffed Liver with creamed potatoes and broad beans and then have a Fruit Cobbler.

SHEPHERD'S PIE

Ingredients

600 g potatoes
2–3 tbsps. milk
25 g margarine
Salt and pepper
1 large onion
25 g dripping or lard
1 level tbsp. flour
1 bouillon cube
250 ml water
300 g cold meat, minced

Utensils

A fairly shallow ovenproof dish
Vegetable knife, round-bladed knife, tablespoon, fork or masher, wooden spoon
Saucepan
Chopping board
Frying pan
Measuring jug

1 Heat the oven to 220°C. (425°F.), mark 7. Grease the dish.

2 Peel the potatoes and cut into even-sized pieces. Boil them in salted water (see p. 56) and when cooked, drain off the water and mash the potatoes with a fork or masher. Beat in the milk, margarine, salt and pepper with a wooden spoon until the potatoes are smooth and creamy (picture A).

3 Peel the onion and chop it finely on a chopping board. Melt the fat in a frying pan, add the onion and fry until soft and beginning to brown; stir from time to time to prevent sticking (picture B).

4 Sprinkle in the flour and stir well. Crumble the bouillon cube and stir this in also. Add the water a little at a time, stirring well until it is all thoroughly mixed (picture C). Now stir in the meat; add more salt and pepper if necessary and simmer for 5 minutes.

5 Pour this meat mixture into the greased dish and pile the potato evenly on top (picture D). Smooth the surface with a knife and mark it with a fork.

6 Bake near the top of the oven until the potato is golden-brown. Garnish—for example, with tomato or parsley.

Variations

1 The cold minced meat may be replaced by a large can of corned beef (chopped).

2 A small can of baked beans may be added to the meat.
3 2–3 level tsps. curry powder and 25 g sultanas may be added to the meat.

Would you serve potatoes with Shepherd's Pie? And which other vegetable would you have? Do you think Baked Stuffed Apples would make a good second course?

TOAD IN THE HOLE

Ingredients	Utensils
100 g plain flour	Sieve, mixing bowl
$\frac{1}{2}$ level tsp. salt	Small basin, measuring jug
1 egg	Teaspoon, tablespoon,
250 ml milk and water	wooden spoon
200 g skinless sausages	Shallow ovenproof dish or
	Yorkshire pudding tin

1 Heat the oven to 220°C. (425°F.), mark 7.

2 *Making Batter:* Sift the flour and salt into the bowl. Break the egg and pour into the centre of the flour (picture A).

3 Put 2 tbsps. of milk and water with the egg in the middle of the bowl. Using a wooden spoon and working from the centre, gradually mix in flour from the edges with the egg and milk (picture B) and beat well till smooth.

4 Gradually add 125 ml of the liquid, beating gently until it is all mixed in and the batter is smooth and bubbly. Now stir in remaining liquid (picture C). The batter can then, if you wish, be covered and left for about $\frac{1}{2}$ hour, although quite a good result is obtained if it is used straight away.

5 *Toad in the Hole:* Grease the dish or tin and put in the sausages. Pour in the batter (picture D).

6 Bake at the top of the oven for 40–45 minutes, or until the batter is well risen and golden; don't open the oven door while the batter is cooking. Serve at once, with cabbage and tomatoes (but no potatoes, because batter is so filling). Then have something interesting like Fruit Salad.

YORKSHIRE PUDDING AND POPOVERS

Heat 25 g fat in a Yorkshire pudding tin and pour in batter mixture. Bake it as above for 35–40 minutes, or until well risen and brown. Cut into squares and serve at once, with roast beef.

For Popovers, well grease a tray of patty tins and heat in the oven until the fat melts. Make half the above quantity of batter (still using 1 egg) and two-thirds fill each patty tin, using a jug. Bake the popovers as for Yorkshire Pudding for 20 minutes, till well risen and golden.

PEASANT OMELETTE

Ingredients	Utensils
2 tomatoes	Vegetable knife, fork,
2 cooked potatoes	palette knife
1 small onion	Chopping board
50 g mushrooms	Basin
4 eggs	Heavy frying pan
Salt and pepper	Serving plate
25 g butter	

1 Peel and slice the tomatoes; dice the potatoes; peel and chop the onion; wash and slice the mushrooms.

2 Break eggs into a basin, whisk lightly with a fork until well mixed and add salt and pepper (picture A).

3 Melt butter in pan, add vegetables so that they cover base of pan and cook over a gentle heat (picture B).

4 Heat the grill. Put the serving plate to warm.

5 When vegetables are cooked, pour in egg mixture (picture C); continue cooking, shaking pan occasionally.

6 As soon as mixture sets and is lightly browned underneath (picture D), put under hot grill till golden on top.

7 Turn omelette on to hot plate and serve at once, with salad. (This is sufficient for 2 people.)

The recipe above is a variation of the " Spanish " omelette, which traditionally also includes chopped green peppers. The tomato, potato, onion and mushroom filling may be replaced by any other savoury mixture you like.

BAKED OMELETTE

100 g bacon, rinded	4 eggs
$\frac{1}{2}$ a small onion	125 ml milk
1 tbsp. chopped parsley	Salt and pepper
2 level tsps. plain flour	100 g Cheddar cheese

1 Heat the oven to 180°C. (350°F.), mark 4.

2 Chop the bacon, fry until crisp and transfer to plate.

3 Chop the onion and fry with the flour in the bacon fat. Put the onion and parsley over the base of a fairly shallow ovenproof dish.

4 Break the eggs into a basin, beat lightly, add the milk and some salt and pepper and pour into the dish.

5 Grate cheese and sprinkle over the egg mixture, with the bacon. Bake for 30 minutes.

MEAT PIE

Ingredients	Utensils
1 pkt. (212 g) of frozen puff pastry	Cook's knife, vegetable knife, round-bladed knife, kitchen scissors, tablespoon, fork, skewer
450 g lean stewing beef	
1 sheep's kidney or 100 g streaky bacon	Chopping board
1 small onion	Plate
50 g mushrooms	Saucepan, basin
2 level tbsps. flour	Pastry board, dredger, rolling pin, pastry brush
Salt and pepper	
Meat extract to flavour	Oval pie dish or ovenproof dish with a wide rim
1 egg	

1 Thaw the pastry at room temperature for 2 hours.

2 Cut the meat into even-sized pieces, trimming off any fat and gristle. Skin the kidney, cut away the central core and cut up the kidney. (Or rind and dice the bacon.)

3 Peel and chop onion finely; wash and slice mushrooms.

4 Mix flour with salt and pepper on a plate and toss the meat in this. Put meat, kidney or bacon, onion, mushroom and meat extract in a pan, cover with water and simmer, covered, for 1½ hours, till tender, then cool.

5 Heat the oven to 220°C. (425°F.), mark 7.

6 Roll out the pastry thinly on a floured board, turn the pie dish upside-down on it and with a knife cut out a " lid " 1 cm larger all round than the dish.

7 Cut strips from the remaining pastry, damp the edges of the dish and stick the strips round the edge (picture A).

8 Pour the cooked meat mixture into the dish, with enough gravy to half-cover. Damp the pastry strips and place pastry lid in position, taking care not to stretch it.

9 Press the edges together, then make fine horizontal cuts all round to " flake " them. Using back of knife, pull up edges of pastry at 3 cm intervals, as in picture B.

10 Brush top of pastry with some of the lightly beaten egg. Bake pie near top of oven for about 20 minutes, until pastry is brown, then reduce oven to 170°C. (325°F.), mark 3 and cook for a further 40 minutes, or until the meat is tender when tested with a skewer.

11 The pie can be decorated with pastry leaves; make them by cutting 2 cm wide strips of pastry into diamonds and marking with a central vein. Stick the leaves in the centre of the pie after this has been brushed over with beaten egg, then brush the leaves also with egg.

Boiled or new potatoes and diced turnips and carrots are good with pie; follow by rice pudding and canned fruit.

A

B

CHICKEN CASSEROLE

Ingredients	Utensils
50 g margarine	A large saucepan
4 chicken pieces	Chopping board
4 bacon rashers	Cook's knife, wooden spoon
1 small onion	Ovenproof casserole
50 g mushrooms	
1 level tbsp. flour	
375 ml bouillon cube stock	
Salt and pepper	
1 tbsp. tomato paste	
Parsley to garnish	

1 Heat the oven to 180°C. (350°F.), mark 4.

2 Melt margarine in saucepan and fry chicken until brown.

3 Remove the rind from the bacon and cut the rashers into small pieces. Peel and chop the onion (picture A). Wash and slice the mushrooms. Add the bacon and onion to the pan and fry until lightly browned.

4 Remove chicken, bacon and onion from pan into casserole (picture B). Add flour to fat remaining in saucepan, stir with wooden spoon and cook for 2 minutes.

5 Remove the pan from the heat. Add the stock gradually, stirring all the time (picture C), then add salt and pepper to taste, the tomato paste and sliced mushrooms.

6 Return pan to heat and bring to boil, stirring.

7 Pour this sauce over the ingredients in the casserole (picture D) and cook in the centre of the oven for 1 hour. If preferred, add the chicken, bacon and onion to the saucepan and simmer on top of the stove for 1 hour.

8 Sprinkle the top of the casserole with chopped parsley.

This dish is just right when you have visitors. Bake jacket potatoes in oven with casserole and serve with a knob of butter in each, or try something quite different—boiled rice. Wash 150 g long-grain rice in a sieve under the cold tap.

Put in a saucepan with 250 ml cold water and 1 tsp. salt, put on lid and boil for 15 minutes, taking care not to let it boil over. Keep rice warm in oven (covered, so that it does not dry out) till needed.

Choose a party-type pudding, such as Coffee and Chocolate Flan, to finish the meal.

COOKING CHICKEN JOINTS

BAKED CHICKEN

Ingredients	Utensils
100 g butter or margarine	Ovenproof dish
4 chicken joints	Small basin
1 egg	2 plates
Seasoning	2 forks
$\frac{1}{2}$ pkt. coating crumbs	Greaseproof paper
50 g Cheddar cheese (optional)	Kitchen paper
1 small onion (optional)	Grater
	Pastry brush

1 Heat the oven to 220°C. (425°F.), mark 7. Put the butter in the ovenproof dish and place in the oven to melt.

2 Wash and wipe the chicken joints.

3 Crack the egg into the basin, add seasoning and whisk lightly with a fork, then pour on to a plate.

4 Pour crumbs on to a sheet of greaseproof paper. Grate cheese (if used) on to a plate and mix with crumbs.

5 Put the chicken joints into the egg one at a time and brush well until completely coated.

6 Lift the chicken from the egg with 2 forks (or a knife and fork), allow to drain for a minute, then place in the crumbs. Pull up the sides of the paper so that the crumbs cover the chicken; using your hands, press the crumbs on to the egg, then shake off any loose ones.

7 Place the chicken in the dish and bake towards the top of the oven for 30 minutes. Take the dish from the oven, turn the joints over, return them to the oven and cook for a further 15–20 minutes, or till tender. Drain on absorbent paper, before serving with baked potatoes and mixed diced vegetables.

8 To serve as seen in picture, pile the chicken in a napkin-lined basket and garnish with small rings of onion.

CHICKEN IN SAUCE

Ingredients

4 chicken joints
2 level tbsps. flour
Salt and pepper
50 g butter
1 can of mushroom,
   tomato or celery soup
1 small onion
1 level tsp. dried sage

Utensils

Plate
Tablespoon, teaspoon,
Cook's knife, wooden spoon
Large frying pan and lid
Can opener
Chopping board

1 Wash and wipe the chicken joints.

2 Mix the flour and seasoning on a plate and coat the chicken joints with them.

3 Melt the butter in the frying pan and brown the chicken on both sides in the hot fat.

4 Pour the soup over. Peel the onion and chop finely, then sprinkle the onion and sage over the soup.

5 Cover with a lid or large plate and simmer gently for about 45 minutes, spooning the soup over the chicken from time to time, to keep it moist.

GOLDEN GRILLED FISH

Ingredients

4 pieces of cod or
haddock fillet (or 4 cod
steaks)
100 g Cheddar cheese
50 g margarine
1 level tsp. dry mustard
(optional)
Salt and pepper

Utensils

Small pointed knife, round-
bladed knife, scissors,
wooden spoon
Shallow ovenproof dish
Grater, plate
Basin
Fish slice or palette knife

1 Heat the grill.

2 Wipe and trim the fish; if steaks are used, remove the centre bone with a small pointed knife and trim off the fins with scissors.

3 Grease the ovenproof dish and lay the fish in it (skin side up, if fillets are used).

4 Place the dish under the grill and cook gently for about 5 minutes.

5 Grate the cheese, using the large holes of the grater and collecting the cheese on a plate. Beat the margarine in a basin until soft, then mix in the cheese, mustard and a good sprinkling of salt and pepper.

6 Turn the fish over, using a fish slice or palette knife (picture A), and grill for a further 3 minutes.

7 Spread the fish with the cheese mixture (picture B) and place under a really hot grill for a final 2–3 minutes, until the topping is golden and bubbling.

Fry some crispy golden chips to eat with the fish and serve with green peas. After this dish, would you prefer a light or a filling pudding?

Notes
Always be careful when buying fish to see that it is really fresh. The flesh should be firm and the eyes bright; there should be no unpleasant smell. Your fishmonger will bone

and skin any fish if you ask him. If you yourself have to remove bones or want to cut the fish into pieces, use a really sharp knife, otherwise the flesh will be broken up.

Sometimes fish is very slippery, but if you dip your fingers into salt, you will be able to get a firm grip.

Fish is cooked when it will come readily away from the bone if you press with the back of a knife, or when the flesh looks white and firm.

Wrap up any fish trimmings in newspaper and throw them away quickly, to stop any fishy smell. And for the same reason wash the pans and dishes as soon as possible.

A

B

BAKED STUFFED FISH

Ingredients	Utensils
4 cod steaks	Kitchen scissors, small
1 thick slice of bread	pointed knife, cook's
$\frac{1}{2}$ a lemon	knife, teaspoon, table-
Some parsley or 1 level	spoon, fork
tsp. mixed herbs	Chopping board
Salt and pepper	A fairly shallow ovenproof
50 g margarine	dish
A little milk to mix	Grater
1 level tbsp. packet	Plate, basin
crumbs (optional)	Small saucepan
Parsley sprigs and lemon	Shallow serving dish
wedges to garnish	

1 Heat the oven to 180°C. (350°F.), mark 4.

2 Trim the fins from the fish with scissors and cut out the centre bone with a small pointed knife (picture A). If possible work on a special chopping board, as fish leaves a distinctive smell.

3 Grease the dish and put in the fish (picture B).

4 Rub the bread against the rough side of the grater to form breadcrumbs; grate the rind from the lemon. Wash the parsley (if used) and chop it finely with a cook's knife until there is enough to make 1 level tbsp.

5 Mix the crumbs, lemon rind, parsley or herbs, salt and pepper in a basin. Melt half the margarine in the small pan and stir into the crumb mixture with a fork (picture C). If necessary add a little milk and stir until the stuffing sticks together.

6 Divide the stuffing between the fish steaks, filling the holes left by the central bones (picture D). Put the remaining margarine in small pieces over the fish and if liked sprinkle with the packet crumbs.

7 Bake in the centre of the oven for about 20 minutes, or until the fish is creamy white and tender.

8 Lift on to the serving dish and garnish with sprigs of parsley and wedges of lemon.

As vegetables, serve creamed potatoes and whole tomatoes that have been baked in the oven in an ovenproof dish with the fish; for the sweet, choose a crunchy pudding that can be baked, such as Fruit Crisps. (Why a crunchy sweet?)

A

B

C

D

FISH PIE

Ingredients	Utensils
450 g potatoes	Cook's knife, vegetable
Salt and pepper	knife, teaspoon, table-
450 g haddock fillet	spoon, wooden spoon,
(skinned by fishmonger)	can opener, fork or
$\frac{1}{2}$ an onion, peeled	masher
50 g streaky bacon	Saucepan and lid
50 g margarine	Chopping board
40 g flour	Frying pan
1 can of tomatoes	Casserole dish
2–3 tbsps. milk	Sieve

1 Peel the potatoes thinly. Put in a saucepan, cover with cold water and add 1 tsp. salt. Bring to the boil, then simmer until tender—20–30 minutes.

2 Heat the oven to 190°C. (375°F.), mark 5.

3 Cut the fish in 5 cm squares. Chop the onion finely (picture A). Rind the bacon and chop into strips. Melt 25 g margarine in a frying pan, add the onion and fry gently for 10 minutes, without colouring. Add the bacon and fish and fry for a further 5 minutes (picture B).

4 Stir in the flour until well mixed, then add the canned tomatoes (picture C). Bring to the boil, stirring, add salt and pepper to taste and pour into the casserole.

5 When the potatoes are cooked, drain in a sieve, return them to the pan, mash and add a little milk, the rest of the margarine and some salt and pepper. Beat with a wooden spoon over a gentle heat until smooth and creamy.

6 Pile the potatoes on top of the fish (picture D), level the surface with a knife and mark a pattern with a fork.

7 Bake at the top of the oven for 30 minutes, till golden.

As there is potato in the pie, you need only a green vegetable such as spinach or French beans as accompaniment. While the pie is in the oven you could make some Apple Fritters.

Haddock (or cod) fillet also makes a good curry. Fry 1 chopped onion in 50 g butter until golden and add 2 skinned and quartered tomatoes. Cut the fish into 5 cm pieces, sprinkle with 2 level tsps. curry powder and fry gently in the pan until golden-brown, then add a pinch of salt and a pinch of sugar. Cover with a lid and cook gently for 10 minutes. Serve with boiled rice.

VEGETABLES

CABBAGE Wash well under a fast-running cold tap, if possible, or in a basin of cold water. Cut in half, using a cook's knife on a chopping board. Cut out the hard centre stem, then place cut side down on the board and slice thinly (picture A). Meanwhile, boil about 5 cm of water in a large saucepan and add 1 level tsp. salt. Put in the cabbage, cover with a lid and boil rapidly until the cabbage is just tender—about 10–15 minutes. Drain really well, stir in a knob of butter and a sprinkling of pepper or nutmeg and serve at once.

SPROUTS Wash well in a basin of cold water, then remove any discoloured outer leaves with a small sharp knife (picture B). Cut a cross in the stem of each sprout to help the heat penetrate. Cook in boiling salted water as for cabbage, allowing about 15–20 minutes. Drain well, stir in a knob of butter and serve at once.

CAULIFLOWER (*Whole*) Wash well and remove any coarse outer leaves (though a few small leaves can be left at the base of the stem). Cut a fairly deep cross in the stem to allow the heat to penetrate (picture C) and cook in boiling salted water as for cabbage. Allow 20–30 minutes, depending on the size of the cauliflower, until it is just tender. Drain well and serve glazed with butter or coated with a cheese sauce (see p. 152: for a white sauce, omit cheese and mustard).

CAULIFLOWER (*Florets*) If preferred, cauliflower can be broken into sprigs or florets before cooking; the cooking time can then be reduced to about 15–20 minutes.

PEAS Shell the peas and cook in boiling salted water (adding 1 level tsp. sugar and a sprig of mint) for about 10–20 minutes, or until tender, depending on the size and age of the peas.

FRENCH OR RUNNER BEANS " Top and tail ", using a small, sharp knife; if they are at all stringy, cut a thin strip from each side (picture D). Cut diagonally into thin pieces and cook in boiling salted water for about 20 minutes, or until tender.

CARROTS (*Old*): Peel thinly with a small, sharp knife or potato peeler over a plate. Cut into rounds if the carrots are small, into dice or strips if large. Put into a pan, cover with salted water, bring to the boil and simmer for about 30 minutes, or until tender. Drain well and stir in a knob of butter and a sprinkling of pepper.

CARROTS (*New*): Wash them in cold water, then scrape off skins with a small, sharp knife. Cut into rings or leave whole if small. Cook as above. Serve glazed with a little butter and sprinkled with chopped parsley or mint.

A   B

C   D

POTATOES

BOILED POTATOES (*Old*) Peel thinly with a small, sharp knife or vegetable peeler, collecting the peelings on a plate and placing the prepared potatoes in a bowl of water so that they will not discolour; if necessary, cut them into even-sized pieces. Put in a pan, cover with cold water and add 1 level tsp. salt. Bring to the boil, then lower heat and simmer for 20–30 minutes (depending on size) until soft but unbroken; drain well. Sprinkle with chopped parsley or toss in a little butter.

(*New*) Place in a bowl of cold water, then scrape with a small, sharp knife, catching the peelings on a plate. Cook as for old potatoes, but allow only about 20 minutes. Toss them in a little butter and sprinkle with chopped parsley.

MASHED POTATOES Boil old potatoes as above and drain well. Return them to the pan and break up with a fork or potato masher until smooth and free from lumps.

CREAMED POTATOES Boil, drain and mash some old potatoes, then add 15 g butter, 3–4 tbsps. milk and some seasoning. Return pan to a gentle heat and beat well with a wooden spoon until potatoes are white, smooth and fluffy. Pile into a serving dish, mark surface with a fork and garnish with parsley (picture opposite).

POTATOES BAKED IN THEIR JACKETS Choose round, even-sized potatoes. Scrub well and prick the skin with a fork. Place near top of a fairly hot oven 200°C. (400°F.), mark 6 and cook for about 1 hour, or until they feel soft. Cut a cross in the skin with a sharp knife, squeeze potato to open up cut slightly and just before serving put in a good knob of butter and some seasoning (picture opposite).

ROAST POTATOES Peel some old potatoes, cut into even sized pieces and boil for 10 minutes, then drain well. Meanwhile heat the oven to 220°C. (425°F.), mark 7 and melt 50 g dripping or lard in a shallow tin. Add the potatoes and spoon the fat over them. Bake near the top of the oven for 20 minutes, then turn the potatoes over and bake for a further 20 minutes or until crisp, golden and soft inside (test with a skewer). Drain on kitchen or absorbent paper and serve at once, in an uncovered dish or around the joint, sprinkled with a little salt.

CHIPPED POTATOES Peel some even-sized fairly large old potatoes; cut into slices about 1 cm thick, then cut these slices into strips about 1 cm wide. (Several slices can be placed on top of one another to make the second cutting process quicker.) Meanwhile half-fill a deep fat fryer with lard or oil and heat it for 10–15 minutes. Put in a test chip—when this rises to the surface bubbling rapidly, the fat is hot enough. Put the chips into the basket and lower gently into the fat. Cook quickly for about 5–10 minutes (depending on how big the chips are and how full the pan), until crisp and golden, yet soft inside. Drain well and serve at once (picture below).

SAUTÉ POTATOES These are usually made with left-over boiled potatoes. Cut the potatoes into rounds 5 mm thick. Melt 50 g butter or dripping in a frying pan; when it is hot, add the potatoes and fry until golden on the under-side. Turn them over and cook until the second side browns also. Drain on kitchen or absorbent paper and serve at once, sprinkled with a little salt and some chopped parsley if available.

SALADS

Preparing the Ingredients

LETTUCE Separate the leaves and wash them under a running cold tap or in a bowl of cold water. Pat the leaves dry in a clean tea towel or drain in a sieve or colander.

WATERCRESS Trim the coarse ends from the stalks and place the watercress in cold water, adding 2 tsps. salt.

MUSTARD AND CRESS Trim off the roots and lower part of the stems with scissors and place the leaves in a colander or sieve. Wash (under a fast-running cold tap, if possible), turning the cress over to remove any seeds.

SPRING ONIONS Trim off the root end with a vegetable knife, remove the papery outer skin and trim the green leaves down to about 5 cm (picture A).

RADISHES Trim off root end and leaves, place radishes in cold water and rub well to remove dirt. Leave whole (if small), slice thinly into rings or make into flowers.

SIMPLE RADISH FLOWERS Make 6–8 small, deep cuts, crossing at centre, at stem end (picture B). Leave in cold water for 1–2 hours, till cut parts open to form " petals ".

TOMATOES If they are to be peeled, dip in a pan of boiling water for a minute, then place in a basin of cold water—the skin should then peel off easily. Slice thinly, cut into 6–8 wedges, or treat as below.

TOMATO LILIES Make V-shaped cuts round middle, cutting right to centre, then carefully pull apart (picture C).

CELERY Separate sticks and scrub well in cold water. Slice, chop or make into curls.

CELERY CURLS Cut strips 1 cm wide and 5 cm long. Make cuts along each, close together and to within 1 cm of one end; leave in cold water for 1–2 hours, till they curl.

CUCUMBER Wipe the skin and cut into very thin slices. If you prefer, place the slices in a small dish and cover with a little distilled (white) vinegar; sprinkle with salt.

To make Cucumber Cones, cut each slice from centre to rim, then wrap one cut edge over the other (picture D).

CABBAGE Wash a few leaves in cold water and soak for about ¼ hour (adding 2 tsps. salt if there is any sign of greenfly). Drain well, then chop finely with a cook's knife or grate them, using the large holes on the grater. Cabbage is most often used in a salad of the cole slaw type—see Golden Slaw on next page.

BEETROOTS These can be bought ready cooked. Peel thinly, then dice or grate. Put in a small dish, sprinkle with salt and pepper and cover with vinegar.

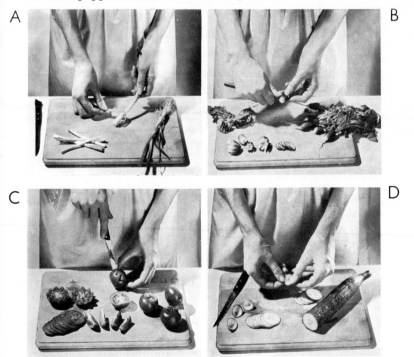

A   B
C   D

MIXED SALAD

Ingredients

4 eggs
A bunch of radishes
A bunch of spring onions
1 lettuce
A bunch of watercress
A tray of mustard and cress
4 tomatoes; 1 beetroot
½ a cucumber
Salad cream

Utensils

Small saucepan
Basin
Vegetable knife
Plates
Colander
Flat serving dish
Small jug

1 Half-fill the saucepan with cold water, put in the eggs, bring to the boil and boil for 10 minutes. Remove from the heat and immediately plunge the eggs into cold water. Remove the shells.

2 Wash the radishes and cut into " lilies ".

3 Wash and trim the spring onions.

4 Wash and drain the lettuce, watercress and mustard and cress and arrange them on the serving dish.

5 Slice the tomatoes, beetroot, cucumber and eggs.

6 Arrange all the ingredients attractively on the dish (see picture) and serve with a jug of salad cream.

GOLDEN SLAW

Ingredients

1 small firm cabbage
500 g red apples
200 g cheese
Salt and pepper
125 ml mayonnaise
1 tbsp. prepared mustard
A little sugar

Utensils

Vegetable knife
Chopping board
Mixing bowl
Tablespoon, fork
Salad bowl

1 Remove and discard the outer leaves of the cabbage. Wash the heart well, shred it finely and put into the bowl.

2 Wipe, core and dice apples, then add to cabbage.

3 Dice the cheese, put this also into the bowl, sprinkle with salt and pepper and mix gently.

4 Mix the mayonnaise and mustard and stir into the vegetables, tossing gently until all pieces are well coated.

5 Serve in the salad bowl, sprinkled with a little sugar.

FRUIT, NUT AND CHEESE SALAD

Ingredients	Utensils
200 g soft cheese	Basin
1 tbsp. stoned raisins	Wooden spoon
1 lettuce	Small saucepan
4 canned peach halves	Flat serving dish
4 walnut halves	
Cucumber and watercress	

1 Beat the cheese in a basin with a spoon until smooth.

2 Boil a little water in the pan, drop in the raisins and allow them to soak for 2 minutes, until soft. Drain well, cool, then mix with the cheese.

3 Wash the lettuce, drain well and arrange on the flat dish in 4 portions. Top each with a peach half, piled with cheese and raisin mixture and decorated with a walnut half. Garnish with sliced cucumber and sprigs of watercress.

MEAT LOAF

Ingredients	Utensils
1 onion	450-g loaf tin
15 ml oil	Chopping board
225 g minced beef	Cook's knife
225 g sausage-meat	Wooden spoon
25 g fresh breadcrumbs	Frying pan
5 ml mixed herbs	Mixing bowl
Salt and pepper	Aluminium foil
1 egg	

1 Heat the oven to 180°C. (350°F.), mark 4.

2 Grease the 450-g loaf tin.

3 Skin and chop onion. Heat the oil in the frying pan and fry onion until it is golden brown.

4 Combine onion with minced beef, sausage-meat, breadcrumbs, herbs and seasoning.

5 Lightly beat the egg and pour into meat mixture, mix well until smooth.

6 Place this mixture into the prepared tin, cover with aluminium foil and cook for $\frac{3}{4}$–1 hour.

7 Allow the loaf to cool in the tin, turn out and slice before serving.

The sweet course rounds off a main meal. As well as adding interest and variety to the meal, it can help supply the necessary daily nutrients in the form of protein in milk puddings, soufflés and mousses, carbohydrates in sponges, pancakes and pastry and vitamins and minerals in fruit.

When choosing the sweet course consider what it is following. Choose something crisp if the first course is soft in texture, something fresh if the main course is rich and something substantial if the first course is very light.

SEMOLINA PUDDING

Ingredients	Utensils
500 ml milk	Saucepan
40 g semolina	Wooden spoon
40 g sugar	Serving dish

1 Pour the milk into a saucepan and bring to simmering point—that is, until it begins to bubble round the edge.

2 Sprinkle the semolina over surface of milk, stir with a wooden spoon and continue heating until milk boils.

3 Reduce heat and add sugar, then cook gently, stirring from time to time, for 15–20 minutes, or until pudding is thick and the grains clear. Pour into a serving dish.

4 Alternatively, cook pudding for 5 minutes after milk has boiled, pour into a greased ovenproof dish and bake in a 180°C. (350°F.), mark 4 oven for 20–30 minutes.

Variations

Orange or Lemon: Add the grated rind of an orange or lemon with the milk when making the pudding.

Fruit: Stir in 25 g stoned raisins or sultanas and 25 g cut-up glacé cherries or peel as soon as the pudding thickens.

Chocolate: Blend 25 g cocoa with a little of the milk before adding to the pudding.

BLANCMANGE

Ingredients	Utensils
60 ml cornflour	Basin, saucepan
30–60 ml sugar	Wooden spoon
568 ml milk	Tablespoon
A strip of lemon rind	600-ml jelly mould or 4 individual glasses

1 Mix the cornflour with the sugar in a basin with a little of the milk. Stir with a wooden spoon until the mixture is smooth (picture A).

2 Boil the remaining milk and lemon rind in a pan. Do not have too high a heat or the milk will burn on the base of the pan, and watch it all the time, as it boils very quickly.

3 Strain the milk on to the cornflour stirring with a wooden spoon to prevent lumps forming (picture B).

4 Return the mixture to the pan and bring gently to the boil, stirring until it is thick, smooth and shiny (picture C).

5 Rinse out the mould with water, quickly pour in the cornflour and leave in a cool place to set for about $1\frac{1}{2}$–2 hours.

6 Loosen edges of mould with fingers (picture D). Cover with an upturned plate then turn plate and mould the other way up shaking mould gently until the mould slides on to the plate.

ORANGE MOULD
Substitute orange rind for lemon rind.

CHOCOLATE MOULD
Mix 15 ml cocoa with the blended cornflour *or* add 50 g melted chocolate to the cooked mixture. Omit the lemon and add a few drops of vanilla.

COFFEE MOULD
Add 15–30 ml coffee essence or 5–10 ml instant coffee powder to the cooled mixture. Omit the lemon rind.

Variations

1 Make up 2 lots of cornflour mould, eg. chocolate and orange, using half quantities in each case. Pour alternate layers into a wetted mould or glasses.

2 Add 25 g chopped walnuts and 25 g raisins to cornflour mixture and stir in.

3 Place 15 ml jam, or drained canned fruit in the bottom of individual glasses and pour the cornflour mixture on top. You can make layers if you wish by repeating this until the glass is full.

A

B

C

D

BAKED RICE PUDDING

Ingredients	Utensils
40–50 g rice	A fine sieve
A small knob of butter	Pie dish, baking tray
25 g sugar	Tablespoon
500 ml milk	
Nutmeg	

1 Heat the oven to 150°C. (300°F.), mark 2.

2 Wash the rice in the sieve and drain well.

3 Grease the pie dish, place on a baking tray and put in the rice (picture A). Add sugar and milk and stir well.

4 Sprinkle a little ground or grated nutmeg on top of the pudding (picture B) and place it in centre of oven. Cook for 2–2½ hours or until it is creamy, with soft grains and a golden skin. (Stir twice during the first hour, so that the rice is well mixed with the milk.)

5 Rice pudding can also be cooked gently in a saucepan on top of the stove for about 1½ hours.

6 Cook tapioca or cut macaroni in the same way.

A

B

STUFFED BAKED APPLES

Ingredients	Utensils
4 even-sized cooking apples	A shallow ovenproof dish
75–100 g mixed dried fruit	Chopping board
25 g demerara sugar	Apple corer
25 g butter	Vegetable knife
30 ml water	Teaspoon

1 Heat the oven to 200°C. (400°F.), mark 6.

2 Wash the apples.

3 Hold the apples firmly on a board and cut out the core with an apple corer. Make a cut through the skin round the middle of each apple.

4 Put the apples in the dish and fill the centre holes with the dried fruit and sugar using a teaspoon. Place small knob of butter on each apple. Pour the water into the dish around the apples.

5 Bake in the centre of the oven, until the fruit is tender but not "fallen", about 30–40 minutes.

SIMPLE APPLE CHARLOTTE

Ingredients

450 g cooking apples
½ a small white loaf
75 g shredded suet
75 g Demerara sugar
1 lemon
25 g butter

Utensils

A pie dish or any ovenproof
 dish
Potato peeler, vegetable
 knife, tablespoon, skewer
Bowl
Grater, plate
Basin
Lemon squeezer
Baking tray

1 Heat oven to 180°C. (350°F.), mark 4. Grease dish.

2 Peel the apples, cut in quarters and remove the cores, then slice them thinly. Drop the slices into a bowl of water, so that they do not discolour (picture A).

3 Cut the bread into thick slices and rub it against the rough side of a grater which is standing on a plate, to form breadcrumbs.

4 Mix the crumbs with the suet and sugar in a basin.

5 Grate the rind from the lemon (picture B), then cut the lemon in half and squeeze out the juice. Drain the apples and mix with the lemon rind.

6 Put a layer of apple in the dish. Sprinkle with lemon juice, then add a layer of crumb mixture (picture C).

7 Continue these layers until the dish is full, finishing with a layer of crumbs. Cut the butter into small pieces and scatter over the crumbs (picture D).

8 Put the dish on the baking tray and cook in centre of oven for about 1¼ hours, till the fruit is tender when tested.

Make full use of the oven by starting the meal with something like Savoury Lamb Chops.

Apple Charlotte is a good way of using up bread that has become dry. It is a popular pudding in winter—when served with hot custard it is filling but not stodgy. Other fruits can be used instead of apples—rhubarb (add extra 25 g sugar), plums (cut in half and stone them) or even drained canned fruit (reduce cooking time to $\frac{1}{2}$ hour).

FRUIT SALAD

Ingredients	Utensils
100 g sugar	Saucepan
250 ml cold water	Wooden spoon
1 lemon	Glass dish
A selection of fruits as available (e.g., 2 red apples, 1 banana, 2 oranges, 100 g black grapes)	Cook's knife
	Lemon squeezer
	Chopping board

1 Dissolve the sugar in the water in the pan, stir and bring to the boil. When cool, pour into the glass dish.

2 Cut the lemon in half, squeeze out the juice and add this to the sugar syrup.

3 Prepare the fruits as necessary.

Apples (picture A): Cut into quarters, remove the core and cut each quarter into thin slices. Place at once in the prepared syrup, to prevent the fruit from going brown.

Banana (picture B): Peel, cut into slices about 5 mm thick and place at once in the prepared syrup, to prevent the fruit from going brown.

Oranges (picture C): Peel and remove all the white pith. Then either divide into segments (though these tend to be large) or preferably cut the orange into slices about 5 mm thick across the segments. In either case remove the pips. Place the pieces in the syrup.

Grapes (picture D): Halve, remove pips, put fruit in syrup.

4 If fresh fruit is scarce, canned fruit may be included—for example, a small can of red cherries, apricot halves, peach slices or pineapple chunks; in this case don't make the sugar syrup, but use the liquid from the can.

If the Fruit Salad is made earlier in the day, the flavour has time to develop. It is such an adaptable sweet that it fits into most menus.

FRUIT FOOL

Open a can of fruit (e.g., apricots, raspberries, blackberries) and rub the actual fruit through a sieve, then add enough juice to make 250 ml. Stir in 250 ml sweetened custard, mixing well, pour into individual glasses and keep in a cool place. Decorate with whole fruit or a little cream.

A

B

C

D

APPLE CORNFLAKE CRUNCH

Ingredients

Utensils

1 kg cooking apples
50–75 g sugar
40 g butter
2 level tbsps. golden syrup
25 g cornflakes
4–6 tbsps. cream,
  evaporated milk or top of
  the milk

Vegetable knife, tablespoon,
  wooden spoon
Plate
Saucepan
Sieve, 2 basins
4 individual dishes

1 Peel the apples, cut in quarters and remove the cores. Slice each quarter thinly into segments, putting into water to prevent discolouring (picture A). Place in a saucepan, add 2–3 tbsps. water, cover with a lid and simmer gently until the fruit is really soft.

2 Stir in the sugar and pour the apples into a sieve over a basin; rub through with a wooden spoon (picture B). Stir this purée well and pour into 4 individual dishes.

3 Heat butter and syrup gently in the clean saucepan until they melt, then stir in the cornflakes. Mix with a wooden spoon until the flakes are evenly coated (picture C).

4 Pour a thin layer of cream or milk on top of each dish of apple (picture D), then pile the cornflakes on top.

What other fruits could you use for this sweet?

The cornflake crunch topping adds a tasty, crispy finish to several simple sweets—Fruit Fool, Whisked Jelly, Caramel Blancmange, Ice Cream.
Plain crushed cornflakes can replace browned breadcrumbs as a coating for fried foods or as a topping for savoury dishes.

CHOCOLATE ROUGHS

A very easy type of small cake can be made in a similar way to the crunch topping. Break up a 100 g block of chocolate into a basin and stand the basin in a pan of hot water, but take great care not to let the chocolate get too hot. When it is just melted and soft, stir in 25 g cornflakes, working lightly so as not to break them up. Using spoon and fork, put heaps of mixture on waxed paper and leave in a cool place until set.

Puffed wheat and rice can also be used in this way.

A

B

C

D

FRUIT CRISP

Ingredients	Utensils
1 large can of fruit (plums, apricots, etc.)	Can opener, round-bladed knife, teaspoon
1 lemon	Basin
75 g self-raising flour	Grater, 2 plates
½ level tsp. salt	Sieve, mixing bowl
50 g margarine	Ovenproof dish
50 g Demerara sugar	Baking tray
25 g desiccated coconut	

1 Heat the oven to 190°C. (375°F.), mark 5.

2 Open the can of fruit and drain off the juice by tipping the contents into a sieve over a basin.

3 Stand the grater on a plate; using the finest holes, grate off the yellow part from the skin of the washed lemon.

4 Sift the flour and salt into the mixing bowl (using a second sieve or making sure the first one is clean and dry).

5 Cut fat into small pieces on a plate and add to flour.

6 Using fingertips, rub in fat till there are no lumps left and mixture is like fine breadcrumbs (picture A).

7 Add sugar, coconut and lemon rind; mix well with knife.

8 Pour the fruit and a little of the juice into an ovenproof dish and sprinkle with the flour mixture (picture B).

9 Place dish on a baking tray and bake near the top of the oven for 20 minutes, or until crisp and golden.

Fruit Crisp will make a quick, easy-to-prepare meal when served after fried sausages, onions, tomatoes and potatoes.

Notes on the Rubbing-in Method
This way of mixing the fat and flour together by using the finger-tips is known as the rubbing-in method. Here are some points to remember when using it:

1 Cut up the fat to make it easier to mix in.

2 Do not use hard fat straight from the refrigerator.

3 On the other hand, do not have the fat too soft, or it will melt as it is rubbed in and will stick to your fingers.

4 Use your finger-tips only for mixing, as they are the coolest part of the hand.

5 Lift your hands well above the bowl when rubbing-in, to allow air to mix with the ingredients as they fall back—this makes the mixture light and keeps it cool.

6 Never use more than half fat to flour.

7 Never go on rubbing after mixture is free from lumps or the fat will soften and make the mixture sticky.

A

B

SYRUP LAYER PUDDING

Ingredients

For the Suetcrust Pastry
200 g self-raising flour
1 tsp. salt
100 g suet
Approx. 8 tbsps. water

For the Filling
4 level tbsps. golden syrup
  (or jam or mincemeat)

Utensils

Steamer or large saucepan
Greaseproof paper, pencil,
  string
$1\frac{1}{2}$ pint pudding basin
Sieve, mixing bowl
Teaspoon, tablespoon,
  round-bladed knife
Measuring jug
Pastry board, dredger,
  rolling pin

1 Boil some water in the base of the steamer or saucepan.

2 Cut double greaseproof paper 5–8 cm larger all round than top of basin. Grease its centre and inside of basin.

3 *Making Suetcrust Pastry:* Sift flour and salt into bowl and stir in suet with a knife. Add most of the water and stir well with the knife (picture A); add remaining water if necessary to make a soft, elastic dough.

4 Flour a board lightly, turn out pastry, knead lightly and divide into 4 pieces. Form each piece into a round and roll it, making first one 8 cm across and each of the others slightly bigger than the last (picture B).

5 Put 1 tbsp. syrup in basin; add smallest pastry round, then more syrup (picture C) and next smallest round. Repeat till both are used up, finishing with largest round.

6 Cover basin as described in note no. 3 (picture D). Put into steamer or pan and cook for $1\frac{1}{2}$ hours—make sure water doesn't boil away. Turn out, serve with custard.

Rules for steaming:

1 Use a large saucepan or a special steamer. When using a saucepan, have the water half-way up the basin, which should stand on a cloth or something similar on base of pan. In a steamer the water should two-thirds fill bottom container.

2 The water should always be boiling rapidly. Check often and keep a kettle boiling to refill pan as necessary.

3 Cover a steamed pudding tightly with a double thickness of greased greaseproof paper or aluminium foil, so that steam cannot reach the pudding and make it soggy.

4 Fill basin only two-thirds full to let pudding rise.

A

B

C

D

BAKED JAM ROLL

Ingredients	Utensils
150 g self-raising flour	Baking tray
$\frac{1}{2}$ level tsp. salt	Sieve, mixing bowl
75 g shredded suet	Round-bladed knife,
Water to mix	teaspoon
Jam or mincemeat	Jug or measuring jug
	Pastry board, dredger,
	rolling pin, pastry brush
	Greaseproof paper

1 Heat the oven to 200°C. (400°F.), mark 6; grease a baking tray.

2 Sift flour and salt into the bowl. Stir in suet, then add water a little at a time (picture A), till the mixture sticks together to form a soft, elastic dough.

3 Turn the dough on to a floured board and knead lightly. Flatten and shape into an oblong, then roll out into a larger oblong, making the pastry 1 cm thick.

4 Spread the pastry generously with jam or mincemeat to within 1 cm of the edge (picture B).

5 Brush the edges of the pastry with water and roll up as tightly as possible, starting from one short end (picture C). Pinch the edges firmly together.

6 Grease well a double sheet of greaseproof paper and wrap the roll in this, pinning or folding the ends under (picture D).

7 Place on the baking tray and bake in the centre of the oven for about 1 hour, or until golden and crisp.

Cook Steak and Tomato Casserole at the bottom of the oven at the same time, so making full use of the heat.

Jam Roll can also be steamed—wrap it in 2 layers of greased greaseproof paper, tying up the ends of the paper to stop any moisture getting in, and steam for $2\frac{1}{2}$ hours.

SAVOURY ROLL

Make as for Baked Jam Roll, but replace the jam filling by the following meat mixture:
200 g minced meat, 100 g rinded and chopped streaky bacon, 1 finely chopped onion, 1 tsp. mixed herbs and salt and pepper to taste, bound with 1 beaten egg.

A

B

C

D
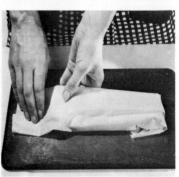

FRUIT COBBLER

Ingredients	Utensils
600 g plums	Saucepan, measuring jug
125 ml water	Pie dish, ovenproof dish
100 g sugar	Sieve, mixing bowl, plate
200 g self-raising flour	Round-bladed knife, tea-
$\frac{1}{4}$ level tsp. salt	spoon, tablespoon, fork
50 g margarine	Basin, pastry board, flour
50 g sugar	dredger, rolling pin
1 egg	2-inch (5 cm) round cutter
1–2 tbsps. milk	Pastry brush
	Baking tray

1 Place the plums in a saucepan with the water and cover with a lid. Simmer gently until the fruit is soft but still whole.

2 Turn the fruit into a dish, cut each plum open and remove the stone. Mix the fruit with the sugar and pour into an ovenproof dish.

3 Heat the oven to 220°C. (425°F.), mark 7.

4 Sift the flour and salt into a mixing bowl.

5 Cut fat into small pieces on a plate. Add it to the mixing bowl and rub it in until the mixture is free from lumps and looks like fine breadcrumbs. Stir in the sugar.

6 Break the egg into a basin and whisk with a fork. Using the knife, stir into the rubbed-in ingredients 1 tbsp. at a time, until the mixture begins to stick together; add some milk if necessary.

7 Collect the mixture together with one hand and knead lightly into a smooth, fairly soft dough.

8 Turn it on to a lightly floured board and roll out 1 cm thick. Cut into 5 cm rounds and place these "scones" on the fruit in a circle, slightly overlapping one another, round the edge of the dish (picture A).

9 Brush the tops of the rounds with a little milk (picture B), place the dish on a baking tray and bake near the top of the oven for 10–15 minutes, or until the rounds are golden-brown, well-risen and firm to the touch.

This is a very filling pudding, so would go well with Golden Grilled Fish, which is a light first course.

Could you use canned fruit in this way?

The cobbler topping can also be used on a casserole to make the dish more satisfying. Make up the scones as above, omitting the sugar, and arrange them on top of the casserole 20 minutes before the end of the cooking time.

JAM TART

Ingredients

100 g plain flour
½ level tsp. salt
50 g lard (*or* 25 g lard
 and 25 g margarine)
20 ml cold water
3–4 rounded tbsps. jam
 (or other preserve)

Utensils

Sieve, mixing bowl
Plate, jug
Round-bladed knife,
 teaspoon, tablespoon
Pastry board, flour dredger,
 rolling pin, pastry brush
7-inch (18 cm) metal plate
Baking tray

1 Heat the oven to 220°C. (425°F.), mark 7.

2 Sift the flour and salt into a mixing bowl.

3 Cut the fat into small pieces on a plate and add it to the flour in the bowl.

4 Using the fingertips only, rub the fat into the flour until there are no lumps left and the mixture looks like crumbs.

5 Add water 2 tsps. at a time, stirring with the knife until the ingredients begin to stick together.

6 Using one hand, collect the mixture together and knead lightly to make a smooth, firm dough (picture A).

7 Place the dough on a floured board and flatten and shape it into a round. Roll it out into a round about 5 mm thick and slightly larger than the metal plate, turning it after each rolling to keep the shape and prevent sticking (picture B).

8 Lift the pastry, supporting it well (picture C) and place on the plate, easing it to follow the shape of the plate, but without stretching it.

9 Holding the plate up, cut off any extra pastry (picture D), then make 3 cm cuts evenly round edge of tart, damp with water and fold over each piece to make a triangle.

10 Spread jam evenly over the centre of the pastry.

11 Place the tart on a baking tray and bake near the top of the oven for 15–20 minutes, or until the pastry is golden.

Vary the filling sometimes by using lemon curd or marmalade instead of jam; another good filling is made by melting 3–4 tbsps. golden syrup in a small pan and stirring in 2 tbsps. fresh white breadcrumbs or crushed cornflakes.

Shepherd's Pie, followed by Jam Tart, is a quick, easy meal.

FRUIT PIE

Ingredients	Utensils
600 g cooking apples	Potato peeler, vegetable
50 g lard (*or*	knife, round-bladed knife,
25 g lard and 25 g	fork
margarine)	Basin, plate, oval pie dish
100 g plain flour	Sieve, mixing bowl, jug
$\frac{1}{2}$ level tsp. salt	Pastry board, flour dredger,
Cold water to mix	rolling pin, pastry brush
100 g sugar	Tablespoon, teaspoon,
4–6 cloves *or* 1 level tsp.	skewer
ground cinnamon	Baking tray

1 Heat the oven to 220°C. (425°F.), mark 7.

2 Peel apples thinly, cut each in four and remove cores. Leave the apples in a basin, covered with water.

3 Cut up the fat and rub it into the sifted flour and salt, until the mixture is like fine, even breadcrumbs.

4 Add water, 2 tsps. at a time, till mixture sticks together; using one hand, knead into a smooth, firm dough.

5 Place the pastry on a floured board, flatten, then roll out about 5 mm thick and into an oval 3 cm larger all round than the top of the pie dish.

6 Turn the dish upside-down on the pastry and draw the knife round it, cutting 1 cm away from the edge of the dish (picture A).

7 Damp the edge of the dish and cover with strips cut from the trimmings of the pastry.

8 Slice half the apples into dish, cover with sugar, add cloves or cinnamon, then slice and add remaining apples.

9 Damp the pastry edge and place lid in position, taking care not to stretch it; press edges together. Starting at the side farthest away from you, decorate the edge of the pastry. Holding down the pastry with the back of the first finger, make close horizontal cuts all round edges of pie (picture B); now mark edges with prongs of a fork to give fine scallops.

10 Place the pie on a baking tin and bake near the top of the oven for 10 minutes or until the pastry has set. Turn down the oven to 180°C. (350°F.), mark 4 and continue cooking for a further 20–30 minutes, or until the fruit is tender when tested with a skewer.

Any fresh or canned fruit can be used in a pie. Try two fruits mixed, or add a flavouring, e.g., ginger with rhubarb.

A Fruit Pie is the traditional pudding with a roast dinner.

EGG CUSTARD TART

Ingredients	Utensils
100 g plain flour	Sieve, mixing bowl
A pinch of salt	Round-bladed knife,
50 g lard (*or* 25 g	tablespoon, teaspoon, fork
margarine and 25 g lard)	Pastry board, dredger,
Water to mix	rolling pin
2 eggs	A fairly deep metal or oven-
1 level tbsp. sugar	proof glass pie plate,
250 ml milk	15–18 cm in diameter
Grated or ground nutmeg	Baking tray
	Basin, saucepan, strainer

1 Heat the oven to 220°C. (425°F.), mark 7.

2 Sift flour and salt into mixing bowl. Cut fat into pieces and rub into flour with the finger-tips until the mixture looks like fine breadcrumbs.

3 Add water 2 tsps. at a time, stirring until the mixture sticks together. Using one hand, collect it together to give a firm dough, then knead lightly.

4 Put on a floured board, shape into a round and roll out 3 cm larger all round than pie plate; line plate, taking care not to stretch or crack pastry (picture A).

5 Using a knife, trim off any extra pastry. Damp edges and fold under 1 cm of the pastry all round. (This double edge is less likely to burn.) Using your fingers, crimp the edge. Place dish on a baking tray.

6 Break the eggs into a basin. Whisk lightly with a fork (picture B), then add sugar. Warm the milk slightly in the pan, then pour it on to the sweetened eggs.

7 Pour this custard mixture through a strainer or sieve into the pastry case, taking care not to spill any over the edge nor to fill the case too full (picture C).

8 Sprinkle with a little nutmeg (picture D) and bake in centre of oven for 10–15 minutes, or until pastry is set, then reduce heat to 170°C. (325°F.), mark 3 and cook for a further 20–30 minutes, or until custard is set.

For individual tartlets, line patty tins with pastry, prick, fill and bake at 220°C. (425°F.), mark 7, for 15 minutes.

Serve after a filling first course like Hot-pot.

PEACH FLAN

Ingredients	Utensils
100 g plain flour	Sieve, mixing bowl, plate
$\frac{1}{2}$ level tsp. salt	Teaspoon, round-bladed
50 g margarine	knife, fork, can opener,
1 level tsp. sugar	wooden spoon
1 egg	3 basins
1 medium-sized can of	Pastry board, dredger,
peaches	rolling pin, cooling tray
3 level tsps. arrowroot or	Flan ring, baking tray
cornflour	Greaseproof paper and
	baking beans
	Measuring jug, saucepan

1 Heat the oven to 200°C. (400°F.), mark 6.

2 *Flan Pastry:* Sift flour and salt into a bowl.

3 Cut up fat and add to flour. Rub in, using fingertips, until mixture looks like breadcrumbs; stir in sugar.

4 Separate egg and add yolk to the rubbed-in ingredients, stirring with a knife until mixture begins to stick together and adding a little cold water if necessary.

5 Using one hand, collect mixture into a firm dough; knead lightly till smooth. Form into a round on a floured board and roll out 5 cm larger all round than flan ring.

6 Place flan ring on baking tray, then carefully lift pastry and place over centre of ring. Lower pastry into ring, taking care not to stretch it and pressing well into place up the fluted sides (picture A).

7 Pass rolling pin across top of ring to cut away any extra pastry (picture B); prick bottom of flan.

8 Put greaseproof paper in case, fill with baking beans (picture C) and bake near top of oven for about 15 minutes, or till pastry is set. (This is called baking blind.)

9 Remove beans and paper (picture D) and continue cooking until pastry is golden. Cool on a wire tray.

10 Drain the peaches in a clean sieve over the basin and arrange the fruit in a pattern in the flan case, filling it well.

11 Measure 125 ml juice and blend this gradually with arrowroot or cornflour. Pour into pan and bring slowly to boil, stirring until it thickens and clears.

12 Pour this glaze evenly over fruit and allow to cool.

CHOCOLATE AND COFFEE FLAN

Ingredients

For the Pastry
100 g plain flour
A pinch of salt
50 g lard (*or* 25 g lard and
  25 g margarine)
Water to Mix

For the Filling
25 g cornflour
2 level tbsps. cocoa
1–2 level tsps. instant
  coffee powder
375 ml milk
25 g margarine
100 g sugar
Grated chocolate or a few
  chopped walnuts for
  decoration

Utensils

Sieve, mixing bowl
Plate
Round-bladed knife,
  teaspoon, tablespoon, fork,
  wooden spoon
Pastry board, dredger,
  rolling pin
A 7-in (18 cm) ovenproof
  glass or metal pie plate
Greaseproof paper, baking
  beans
Cooling rack
Measuring basin
Saucepan
Grater

1 Heat the oven to 220°C. (425°F.), mark 7.

2 Sift the flour and salt into a mixing bowl. Cut up the fat and rub it into the flour until the ingredients look like fine breadcrumbs.

3 Add water 2 tsps. at a time, stirring with a round-bladed knife until the mixture sticks together. Collect into a dough and knead lightly.

4 Turn it on to a floured board, shape with the hands into a round and roll out to a round 3 cm larger all round than the pie plate. Line the plate with the pastry, taking care not to stretch it.

5 Trim off the edges of the pastry, damp the border, turn under 1 cm all round, then crimp with the fingers. Bake blind (see p. 90) at the top of the oven for about 20 minutes; cool on the rack.

6 Blend the cornflour, cocoa and coffee with 2 tbsps. of the milk in basin. Heat remaining milk, watching it all the time.

7 When milk boils, pour it into the basin, stirring all the time (picture A). Return mixture to pan and bring to the boil, stirring with a wooden spoon. Add the margarine and sugar and beat until smooth and shiny.

8 Pour the filling into the cooked pie case (picture B) and leave to set, then sprinkle with the chocolate or the walnuts.

For a rather special meal, serve Pork and Pineapple before this delicious flan.

A

B

APRICOT AMBER

Ingredients

For the Pastry
100 g plain flour
A pinch of salt
50 g lard (*or* 25 g lard
  and 25 g margarine)
Water to mix

For the Filling
1 large can of apricots
  (or other canned or
  stewed fruit)
2 eggs
50 g butter
50 g caster sugar

Utensils

Sieve, mixing bowl, plate
Round-bladed knife,
  teaspoon, tablespoon,
  wooden spoon, can opener
Measuring jug
Pastry board, dredger,
  rolling pin, cooling rack
A 7-in (18 cm) shallow pie
  plate or ovenproof dish
Greaseproof paper, baking
  beans
2 basins, 2 cups
Saucepan, whisk

1 Heat the oven to 220°C. (425°F.), mark 7.

2 Sift flour and salt into bowl and rub in cut-up fat.

3 Add water 2 tsps. at a time and mix to a firm dough. Knead lightly.

4 Put dough on a floured board, shape into a round and roll out into a round 3 cm larger all round than pie plate. Line plate with pastry, taking care not to stretch it.

5 Trim off any extra pastry, damp the edges, turn under 1 cm and crimp with the fingers (picture A). Bake blind (see page 90) at top of oven for 20 minutes. Cool on a rack.

6 Open apricots and strain through clean sieve over basin. Put sieve over another basin and push apricots through with a wooden spoon (picture B); add just enough juice to make a thickish pulp.

7 Separate the eggs; melt the butter in a saucepan. Stir the egg yolks and butter into the apricots and pour this mixture into the cooked pastry case (picture C).

8 Reduce oven to 180°C. (350°F.), mark 4 and cook for about 15 minutes, or until the filling is firm.

9 Whisk egg whites in a clean bowl till stiff enough to stand up in peaks. Fold in sugar, using tablespoon, and pile on to filling, covering it completely (picture D).

10 Reduce the oven to 150°C. (300°F.), mark 1 and bake near the bottom until the topping is crisp—about ½ hour.

Serve after a simple first course, like Baked Fish.

QUEEN OF PUDDINGS

Ingredients

2–3 thick slices of bread
  (100 g in weight)
1 lemon
375 ml milk
40 g butter
40 g sugar
2 eggs
2–3 tbsps. raspberry jam
50 g caster sugar

Utensils

A fairly deep ovenproof dish
Knife, tablespoon
Grater, plate
Saucepan
1 large and 1 small basin
Mixing bowl, whisk

1 Heat oven to 170°C. (325°F.), mark 3. Grease dish.

2 Rub the bread against the rough side of a grater (which is standing on a plate), to make breadcrumbs. Weigh out 75 g of the crumbs. Grate the rind from the lemon.

3 Put the milk and butter in the saucepan and the crumbs, lemon rind and sugar in a large basin. Bring the milk to the boil, pour it into the crumb mixture, stir well and leave to cool for about $\frac{1}{2}$ hour.

4 Separate the eggs, putting the whites into a small basin. Stir the yolks into the cooled crumb mixture (picture A). Pour into the greased dish and bake in the centre of the oven until set—about 45 minutes.

5 When the pudding is cooked remove from the oven. Melt the jam in the washed saucepan and put it over the pudding in an even layer (picture B).

6 Put the egg whites in a mixing bowl, whisk until stiff enough to stand up in peaks (picture C), then fold in the caster sugar carefully, using a tablespoon.

7 Pile this meringue evenly on to the pudding, starting from the outside edge of the dish and working inwards, so that the jam is completely covered (picture D).

8 Reduce oven heat to 150°C. (300°F.), mark 1 and bake near top for about ½ hour, till meringue is faintly coloured.

The meringue topping given here may equally well be used on a baked milk pudding. Use 1–2 egg whites and stir the yolks into the actual cereal and milk mixture.

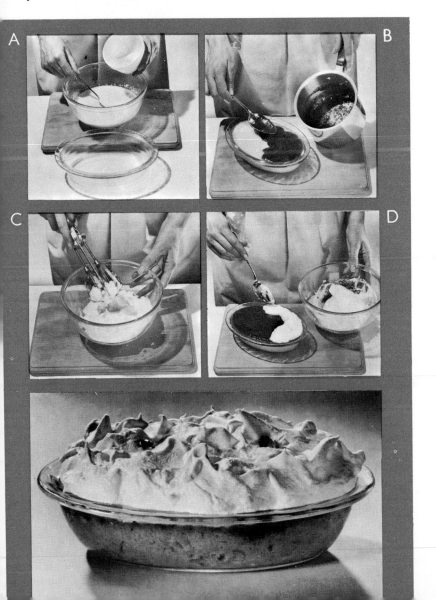

JAM SPONGE PUDDING

Ingredients

2 level tbsps. jam (*or* syrup or marmalade)
125 g self-raising flour
75 g margarine
75 g caster sugar
1 egg
2 tbsps. milk to mix (approx.)

Utensils

Steamer or large saucepan
Greaseproof paper, pencil, scissors, string
$1\frac{1}{2}$-pint pudding basin
Tablespoon, teaspoon, wooden spoon, fork, knife
Sieve, plate
Mixing bowl, basin

1 Boil some water in the steamer or saucepan.

2 Cut a double piece of greaseproof paper 5–8 cm larger all round than basin top. Grease centre of paper and inside of basin (picture A). Put jam in basin.

3 Sift the flour on to a plate.

4 Cream the fat and sugar in the mixing bowl, using a wooden spoon, until mixture is pale, soft and fluffy.

5 Break the eggs into a basin and whisk with a fork until frothy; add 2 tsps. at a time to the fat and sugar, beating well.

6 Fold in half the flour with a tablespoon, then fold in the remaining flour, adding sufficient milk to make a mixture soft enough to drop quite easily from the spoon when this is held above the bowl and shaken.

7 Put mixture in basin (picture B), making sure this is only two-thirds full and levelling top with a knife.

8 Cover basin with greaseproof paper and tie in place. Steam for 2 hours. When pudding is cooked, remove paper, loosen edges of pudding with knife and turn out on dish.

Variations

Omit the jam, syrup or marmalade and replace as follows:

Chocolate: Replace 25 g flour by 25 g cocoa.

Fruit: Clean 100 g dried fruit; sift 1 level tsp. mixed spice with flour. Fold fruit in with flour and spice.

Fruit Cap: Place a layer of well-drained canned fruit in bottom of basin before putting in pudding mixture.

Orange or Lemon: Grate the rind from an orange or lemon and beat in with the creamed mixture.

Individual Puddings: Divide the mixture between 4 small greased tins or basins, cover and steam for $\frac{1}{2}$–$\frac{3}{4}$ hour.

Choose a first course that is cooked on the top of the stove, for example, Ragoût of Liver.

A

B

UPSIDE-DOWN PUDDING

Ingredients	Utensils
1 small can of pineapple rings	A 7-in (18 cm) round cake tin
25 g glacé cherries	Greaseproof paper, pencil, scissors
3–4 level tbsps. golden syrup	Sieve, 2 basins
125 g self-raising flour	Small saucepan
75 g margarine	Plate, mixing bowl
75 g caster sugar	Wooden spoon, fork, teaspoon, tablespoon, round-bladed knife
1 egg	
2–3 tbsps. milk or water	Serving plate

1 Heat the oven to 180°C. (350°F.), mark 4.

2 Place tin on greaseproof paper, draw round it and cut out. Grease tin well, put paper in place and grease it.

3 Open the can of pineapple and pour the contents into a sieve over a basin, to strain off the juice. Arrange the pineapple rings on the base of the cake tin and place a cherry in the centre of each ring.

4 Melt the syrup in a saucepan and pour it gently over the fruit, taking care not to disarrange it.

5 Sift flour on to a plate (using a second sieve or making sure first one is clean and dry). Cream fat and sugar, using a wooden spoon, until pale, soft and fluffy.

6 Break the egg into a basin and whisk with a fork. Add the egg to the creamed fat and sugar 2 tsps. at a time, beating well every time.

7 When all the egg is mixed in, fold in half the flour with a tablespoon. Fold in the remaining flour and add enough of the milk (or water) to give a fairly soft mixture which will drop quite easily from the spoon.

8 Place spoonfuls of the cake mixture evenly over the fruit (picture A), starting from the outside of the tin and working inwards. Level surface of cake with a knife.

9 Bake in the centre of the oven for 40–45 minutes, or until well-risen, golden and firm to the touch.

10 Place upturned serving plate over tin (picture B) and turn both right side up, shaking gently to loosen pudding; peel off paper. Serve pudding with extra melted syrup, the juice from the fruit or some cream.

Canned apricots, peaches or pears can be used instead of the pineapple. When pears are used, replace 25 g of the flour by 25 g cocoa, sifting this with the flour.

This pudding would be good after Ham and Leeks au Gratin.

A

B

FRUIT SPONGE FLAN

Ingredients	Utensils
50 g plain flour plus 2 level tsps.	A 7- or 8-in (18 or 20 cm) sponge flan case
50 g caster sugar plus 2 level tsps.	Teaspoon, tablespoon, whisk, round-bladed knife
2 eggs	Large saucepan, small saucepan, pan stand
400 g fresh raspberries	Mixing bowl
3–4 level tbsps. red-currant jelly	Sieve, cooling tray

1 Heat the oven to 190°C. (375°F.), mark 5. Grease the flan case very well. Sprinkle in 2 tsps. flour and 2 tsps. sugar and shake tin well to coat surface with mixture.

2 Half-fill large saucepan with water, bring this to the boil, then put the pan on the table on a pan stand.

3 Put remaining sugar and eggs in bowl and rest this on top of saucepan. Whisk the mixture until pale, stiff and fluffy (picture A). Remove bowl from top of pan and whisk for a further few minutes, to cool the mixture.

4 Sift the flour on to the whisked mixture; using a tablespoon, fold in the flour very lightly (picture B).

5 Pour the mixture into the prepared tin and bake near the top of the oven for about 20 minutes, or until the flan is firm to the touch, well risen and golden.

6 Loosen edges of flan well with knife (picture C), invert cooling tray over top of tin, then turn right side up and shake gently till flan comes loose; leave to cool.

7 Pick over fruit, removing damaged berries, wash if necessary, then pile fruit in flan case.

8 Put jelly in small pan and heat gently till it melts. Spoon over fruit in a thin, even layer (picture D) or brush it on with a pastry brush. Allow to set before serving the flan.

Glaze: With light-coloured fruit (e.g., peaches, apricots), make a glaze by melting and sieving some apricot jam. For canned fruits a glaze may be made from the juice, thickened as described for Peach Flan, p. 90. For yet another glaze, make up half a packet of jelly in usual way and leave till almost set—use to replace red-currant jelly.

Compare the cost of this Flan with that of a bought one.

A B C D

PANCAKES

Ingredients	Utensils
100 g plain flour	Sieve, mixing bowl
A pinch of salt	Measuring jug
1 egg	Wooden spoon, tablespoon,
250 ml milk and water	palette knife
Lard for frying	Small frying pan
Sugar and lemon wedges	Small basin, 2 plates

1 Sift the flour and salt into the mixing bowl. Make a hole in the centre of the flour and break in the egg.

2 Add 2 tbsps. liquid; working from centre of the bowl, stir until all the ingredients are mixed together, then beat well.

3 Add half remaining liquid a little at a time and beat gently until batter is smooth. Stir in remaining liquid.

4 Heat oven to 130°C. (250°F.), mark $\frac{1}{4}$, to keep first lot of pancakes warm while rest are being cooked.

5 Put a small piece of lard in the frying pan and heat until it begins to " haze "; pour off some into a small basin if necessary, so that the fat just coats the pan.

6 Pour in a little batter, using a jug and tipping pan to cover base thinly—a thick pancake is heavy. (Picture A.)

7 Fry over a moderate heat until golden underneath, shaking pan gently so that it does not stick (picture B).

8 When batter has set on top also, loosen edges of pancake with palette knife and turn the pancake over (picture C) or toss it. Cook until second side is golden.

9 Turn pancake out on to a plate, sprinkle with sugar (picture D), cover with another plate and place in the oven.

10 When pancakes are all cooked, roll each up or fold in four and serve piled, with wedges of lemon or orange.

SAVOURY STUFFED PANCAKES Mix 200 g cooked mince with 1 minced onion and carrot, a little stock and 1 level tsp. mixed herbs; then cook for about 15 minutes.

Make pancakes without sugar. Spread a little filling on each and roll up. Place in a greased ovenproof dish and sprinkle with 50 g grated cheese. Put near top of hot oven 220°C. (425°F.), mark 7, for 10 minutes.

SWEET STUFFED PANCAKES Fill with jam or fruit, etc.

A

B

C

D

PINEAPPLE FRITTERS

Ingredients

Lard or cooking oil
100 g plain flour
½ level tsp. salt
1 egg
125 ml milk and water
1 can of pineapple rings
1 level tbsp. caster sugar
¼ level tsp. ground
cinnamon or ginger

Utensils

A fairly large saucepan or
deep-fat frying pan
Sieve, mixing bowl
Teaspoon, tablespoon,
wooden spoon, can opener,
knife, skewer or fork,
slotted spoon or fish slice
2 basins, measuring jug
2 plates, kitchen paper

1 Heat lard or oil gently in saucepan or deep frying pan—the fat should be 5–8 cm deep.

2 Sift flour and salt into mixing bowl. Break egg into basin and pour into centre of flour.

3 Add 2 tbsps. of the liquid; using a wooden spoon and working from the centre of the bowl, gradually mix the flour from the edges of the bowl with the egg and liquid, then beat well until the mixture is smooth.

4 Add remaining milk gradually, beating well until batter is smooth and will just coat the back of the spoon when this is held above the bowl.

5 Open the can of pineapple and pour the contents into the clean sieve over a basin to drain.

6 Test the fat to see if it is hot enough—when you add a cube of bread, this should brown in 60–70 seconds. Pick up a pineapple ring on a skewer or fork, dip in the batter till well coated (picture A), then drop it gently into the fat. Add another 2–3 rings—do not cook more than this at a time.

7 Turn the fritters once during the cooking and when they are golden, remove from the fat with the slotted spoon or slice and leave to drain on absorbent paper or tissues until quite free from fat (picture B).

8 Mix the sugar and spice and sprinkle on fritters.

Variations

1 Use other fruits such as drained canned apricot or peach halves, mandarin orange sections, peeled and quartered bananas, or apples, peeled, cored and cut into rings.

2 Make savoury fritters—which canned meats do you think would be good used in this way?

Note: Fritters need so much last-minute attention that you must choose for the first course something that needs very little done before it is served—such as Meat Pie.

A  B

LEMON CORNFLAKE FLAN

Ingredients

For the Filling
1 pkt. lemon jelly
375 ml water
1 small can of evaporated
  milk or cream

For the Cornflake Crust
75 g cornflakes
1 level tsp. ground
  cinnamon
50 g margarine
50 g sugar
1 level tbsp. golden syrup

Utensils

A large basin
Measuring jug
Wooden spoon, tablespoon,
  teaspoon, can opener
A large saucepan
A 7-in (18 cm) flan tin or a
  shallow (18 cm) pie plate
  (or any shallow dish)
Whisk
Mixing bowl

1 Divide the jelly into cubes and place in a basin. Boil 125 ml of the water and pour on, stirring until jelly dissolves.

2 Add the remaining 250 ml water, mix well and leave in a cool place.

3 Crush the cornflakes roughly with the hands and mix with the cinnamon (picture A).

4 Heat the margarine, sugar and syrup in a large pan until melted. Allow to boil for 1 minute, then remove from heat and stir in cornflake mixture with a wooden spoon until the flakes are well coated (picture B).

5 Grease the flan tin or pie plate, then line with the corn-flake mixture, pressing it firmly against the sides to give a firm, smooth " crust " (picture C). Leave in a cool place until hard.

6 When the jelly is just beginning to set, turn it into a mixing bowl and whisk until frothy (picture D). Open the can of milk or cream, stir it into the jelly and whisk again until the mixture is thick and fluffy.

7 If the crust was made in a flan tin, remove this carefully and place the crust on a serving plate. If a plate or dish was used, the flan may be served from this. Pile the jelly into the crust just before serving.

The flan case and the filling can be made earlier in the day and left in the refrigerator while you prepare a roast dinner, then assembled just before the last-minute rush.

STRAWBERRY SHORTCAKE

Ingredients

Utensils

200 g self-raising flour
$\frac{1}{4}$ level tsp. salt
75 g margarine
75 g sugar
1 egg
1–2 tbsps. milk
400 g strawberries
3–4 tbsps. sugar for fruit
125 ml double (or
  imitation) cream

An 8-in (20 cm) round
  cake tin
Sieve, mixing bowl
Teaspoon, tablespoon,
  round-bladed knife, fork
Plate, 3 basins
Pastry board, dredger,
  rolling pin
Cooling tray
Colander, whisk

1 Heat the oven to 190°C. (375°F.), mark 5. Grease the sandwich cake tin.

2 Sift the flour and salt into a mixing bowl.

3 Cut fat up small, add to bowl and rub in, using the fingertips, until mixture is free from lumps and looks like fine breadcrumbs; stir in the sugar.

4 Break the egg into a basin and whisk lightly with a fork. Add the egg a little at a time to the mixing bowl, stirring with a knife until the mixture begins to stick together; use a little milk as well if necessary.

5 Using one hand, collect the mixture together and knead lightly into a smooth, fairly firm dough.

6 Turn the dough on to a floured board, form it into a round and roll out until 20 cm across (picture A).

7 Press dough evenly into cake tin (picture B) and bake near the top of oven for 20 minutes, or until golden and firm. Turn cake out of tin on to a cooling tray.

8 Wash strawberries and remove hulls and stems. Keep about a dozen berries whole for decorating; crush rest with a fork in a basin and sprinkle with 2–3 tbsps. sugar.

9 Split cake and place lower half on a plate. Spread with the crushed fruit (picture C) and replace the top.

10 Whisk cream until stiff, stir in remaining sugar and pile on cake (picture D); decorate with whole berries.

Note: Strawberries are the traditional filling, but any soft fruit—raspberries, blackberries, black or red currants and so on—can be used. This is a party-style sweet, so serve it after, say, a chicken first course.

A

B

C

D

APPLE DUMPLINGS

Ingredients	Utensils
200 g plain flour	Baking tray
A pinch of salt	Mixing bowl, sieve
100 g margarine and lard	Plate, jug
mixed	Round-bladed knife,
Water to mix	teaspoon, tablespoon
4 good-sized apples	Pastry board, flour dredger,
50 g sugar	rolling pin, pastry brush
A little milk	15 cm pan lid or saucer
Caster sugar	Apple corer, potato peeler
Small basin

1 Heat the oven to 220°C. (425°F.), mark 7. Grease a baking tray.

2 Use flour, salt, fats and water to make shortcrust pastry—see Jam Tart, p. 84. Divide into 4 portions, roll out each and cut into a 15 cm round with the aid of the lid or saucer

3 Core and peel apples, place one on each round and fill centre with sugar and 1 tsp. water.

4 Moisten edges of pastry with water and carefully gather them to the top of the apple, pressing firmly together.

5 Turn the dumplings over, put on the tray, brush with milk and bake in the centre of the oven for 10 minutes; lower the oven heat to 170°C. (325°F.), mark 3 and cook for a further 30 minutes. Dredge with caster sugar before serving.

TEATIME

The traditional 5 o'clock tea consists of a selection of sandwiches, small cakes, biscuits, fruit or sponge cake. Tea is the usual drink. It can be Indian or China, with milk or lemon.

Choose only one or two foods that are not too substantial because while pleasant, most foods eaten at teatime are fattening and should only be eaten in small quantities. Arrange foods as attractively as possible and remember that contrasting flavours and textures are very important.

SANDWICHES

Pick Your Filling: Here are just a few suggestions—
Flaked salmon, chopped cucumber and salad cream.
Scrambled egg, ketchup and chopped cress or chives.
Chopped corned beef, grated onion and mustard or pickle.
Liver sausage and pickle or sliced or chopped tomato.
Grated cheese, chopped celery and salad cream.
Sardine, lemon juice, chopped tomato or grated onion.
Chopped grilled bacon or cooked ham and scrambled egg.
Sliced cooked sausage and chutney or mustard.
Cream cheese and grated onion or chopped green pepper.
Always popular are such simple fillings as cold beef with thin raw onion slices or horseradish sauce; ham with mustard or cranberry sauce; roast pork with pickle or apple sauce; cheese with chutney or sliced tomato.

SANDWICH-MAKING

1 Prepare filling, making sure it is not crumbly or difficult to eat. Slice meat or poultry thinly; shred, chop or slice salad stuff; use scrambled eggs, not sliced hard-boiled ones.

2 To give moistness, bind filling with salad cream, ketchup or top of milk. Use plenty of seasoning and flavouring— salt, pepper, mustard, chopped chives, chutney.

3 If bread is to be sliced by hand, have it 1 day old. Use a sharp saw-edged knife and cut on a board. When making a lot of sandwiches, you can save time by using ready-cut loaves, unless you need very thin slices.

4 Use thin slices for party or afternoon tea sandwiches, thicker ones for picnics and packed lunches. Cut off the crusts for sandwiches for formal occasions.

5 Place the cut slices of bread in pairs as they come from the loaf, so that they are the same size and the edges match; lay them all out on the table before spreading.

6 Soften butter for easy spreading by leaving it in a warm place for a short time. Spread evenly with a round-bladed knife, taking it right to crusts (picture A).

7 Put filling on half the slices, then cover with the remaining ones—this is quicker than making one sandwich at a time. Use filling generously, taking it right to edges of bread.

8 Press the covering slices firmly in place (picture B). Cut diagonally in halves or quarters, using a sharp knife (not serrated), so as not to tear the bread.

9 To make fancy shapes, cut made sandwiches into strips, diamonds, or tiny squares, after removing the crusts.

10 If sandwiches are made in advance, keep them fresh by wrapping them in foil, polythene, waxed paper or a damp tea towel and putting in a cool larder or in the fridge.

TOASTED SANDWICHES

Instead of bread, use 2 pieces of toast, buttering and filling as usual. Alternatively, toast a sandwich made in the ordinary way.

Some appetising fillings are:

Hot baked beans mixed with crumbled crisply fried bacon
Fried egg and bacon
Friced sliced luncheon meat with slices of tomato and onion
Grilled hamburgers and cheese

A

B

SCONES

Ingredients	Utensils
200 g self-raising flour	Baking tray, cooling rack
$\frac{1}{4}$ level tsp. salt	Sieve, mixing bowl, plate
40 g margarine	Round-bladed knife,
40 g sugar	teaspoon, tablespoon
50 g cleaned currants	Measuring jug
125 ml milk	Pastry board, flour dredger,
	rolling pin, pastry brush
	A 2-in (5 cm) round cutter

1 Heat the oven to 220°C. (425°F.), mark 7. Grease tray.

2 Sift the flour and salt into the mixing bowl.

3 Cut the fat into small pieces and add to flour.

4 Rub in fat with fingertips (picture A) until no lumps are left and mixture looks like fine breadcrumbs.

5 Stir in the sugar and fruit and then add the milk 1 tbsp. at a time (picture B), stirring well with a knife until the mixture begins to stick together.

6 Using one hand, collect the mixture together (picture C) and knead lightly to form a smooth, fairly soft dough.

7 Turn it on to a lightly floured board, form into a flat, round shape and roll out until 3 cm thick.

8 Cut into 5 cm rounds, place on greased baking tray (picture D) and brush tops of scones with a little milk.

9 Bake towards the top of the oven for about 10 minutes, until golden and well risen.

10 Remove to the cooling tray and leave until cold. Serve split in half and buttered.

Variations:

1 For a plain scone, omit the fruit. Plain scones are usually served with jam and sometimes cream.

2 Replace the currants by sultanas, chopped dates or chopped glacé cherries.

3 Leave out the sugar and currants and replace by 50 g grated Cheddar cheese, adding it to the rubbed-in ingredients. Extra grated cheese may be sprinkled on top before the scones are cooked.

Compare the cost of these scones with that of a batch made with a packet mix.

A

B

C

D

DROP SCONES

Ingredients
100 g self-raising flour
15–25 g sugar
1 egg
150 ml milk

Utensils
Frying pan or 'girdle'
Basin, sieve
Wooden spoon
Tablespoon
Palette knife
Cooling rack, tea towel

1 Sieve flour into bowl and mix in sugar.

2 Break in the egg, add half the milk and beat to a smooth batter (picture B).

3 Add the rest of the milk and beat until bubbles rise to the surface.

4 Heat the girdle, pan or hot-plate until the fat is hazing. Wipe the surface with a piece of kitchen paper. Place large tablespoon of batter on surface and cook on one side (picture C). When bubbles appear on the surface of the scone, turn it over with a palette knife (picture D) and cook for another $\frac{1}{2}$–1 minute, or until golden brown.

5 Remove and place on a cooling rack. Cover with a clean tea cloth, while the rest are being cooked.

6 Serve buttered.

These scones may be cooked on a special "girdle", in a heavy frying pan or on a solid hot-plate. Prepare the surface by rubbing with salt on a pad of kitchen paper (picture A); wipe clean and grease the surface very lightly.

A

B

C

D

MINCEMEAT SLICES

Ingredients	Utensils
200 g self-raising flour	Baking tray
¼ level tsp. salt	Sieve, mixing bowl, plate
100 g margarine	Round-bladed knife,
100 g sugar	teaspoon, tablespoon, fork
1 egg	Basin, jug
1–2 tbsps. milk	Pastry board, flour dredger,
3–4 tbsps. mincemeat	rolling pin, pastry brush
1 cooking apple	Grater
1 tbsp. Demerara sugar	

1 Heat the oven to 190°C. (375°F.), mark 5. Grease the baking tray.

2 Sift the flour and salt into the mixing bowl.

3 Cut the fat into small pieces on a plate and rub it into the dry ingredients until the mixture looks like fine bread-crumbs. Stir in the sugar.

4 Break the egg into a basin and whisk with a fork. Add 1 tbsp. at a time to the rubbed-in mixture, until it begins to stick together; add some milk if necessary.

5 Using one hand, collect the mixture together and knead lightly to form a fairly soft dough.

6 Divide into two equal pieces. Place one piece on a floured board and roll out into a 21 cm square, 1 cm thick (picture A); place on the greased baking tray.

7 Spread with mincemeat. Peel and grate the apple on to a plate and sprinkle evenly over mincemeat (picture B).

8 Roll out remaining dough into another 21 cm square (picture C) and cover apple with this, damping edges of both pieces of dough and pressing them together.

9 Brush with milk, sprinkle with Demerara sugar (picture D), bake towards top of oven for 20 minutes, or until golden.

10 When the cake is cold, cut in squares.

SAVOURY CHEESE SLICES are good for a supper or picnic. Omit sugar from the scone mixture and add 75 g finely grated cheese. Chop 1 onion finely, fry in 25 g butter till golden and add 3 rashers of bacon, chopped, and 1 tsp. mixed dried herbs. Use this mixture for the filling and top the slices with 50 g finely grated cheese before baking.

A

B

C

D

FRUIT CAKE

Ingredients	Utensils
200 g dried fruit (currants, sultanas)	Oblong cake tin, 8½ by 4½ in (22 by 11 cm), or a 6-in (15 cm) round cake tin
200 g self-raising flour	
1 level tsp. mixed spice (optional)	Sieve, 2 plates
100 g margarine	Mixing bowl
100 g caster sugar	Wooden spoon, fork or whisk, tablespoon, teaspoon, round-bladed knife
2 eggs	
3–4 tbsps. milk	
2 level tsps. caster sugar for top of cake	

1 Heat the oven to 180°C. (350°F.), mark 4.

2 Grease the sides and base of the cake tin well.

3 Place the fruit in a sieve, sprinkle over it 1 tbsp. of the flour and shake well over a plate (picture A), so that any stalks or bits pass through on to the plate.

4 Sift the flour and spice (if used) on to a plate.

5 Cream the fat and sugar, using a wooden spoon, until the mixture is pale, soft and fluffy.

6 Break the eggs into a basin, whisk with a fork or a whisk until frothy and then add the egg 2 tsps. at a time to the creamed fat and sugar, beating well each time.

7 When all the egg has been added, stir in the fruit, using a tablespoon.

8 Fold in half the flour with a tablespoon, then fold in the remaining flour, adding sufficient milk to make a mixture soft enough to drop quite easily from the spoon when this is held above the bowl and shaken.

9 Put the mixture into the cake tin, levelling the surface with a knife (picture B).

10 Sprinkle the top with 2 tsps. sugar. Bake just below the centre of the oven for about 1¼ hours, or until the cake is well-risen, golden, firm to the touch and beginning to shrink away from the sides of the tin.

CHERRY CAKE Omit the spice, replacing it by the grated rind of 1 lemon or 1 tsp. almond essence, added with the eggs. Replace the dried fruit by 100 g glacé cherries; first roll these in 1 tbsp. flour and cut in quarters.

GINGER CAKE Omit spice and dried fruit. Chop 100 g preserved ginger into small pieces, mix with 1 tbsp. of the flour and fold into mixture last of all. When cake is baked and cold, coat with glacé icing made up with equal amounts of lemon juice and water (p. 142); decorate with ginger.

A   B

COCONUT BUNS

Ingredients

Utensils

50 g self-raising flour
25 g desiccated coconut
25 g glacé cherries
50 g margarine
50 g caster sugar
1 egg

Sieve, plate
Round-bladed knife, fork,
    tablespoon, teaspoon,
    wooden spoon
9 paper baking cases
Baking tray
Mixing bowl, basin
Cooling rack

1 Heat the oven to 190°C. (375°F.), mark 5.

2 Sift the flour on to a plate and mix with the coconut. Cut the cherries in halves.

3 Place paper cases on baking tray, with even spaces between them and none of them too near the edge of the tray.

4 Beat the fat and sugar together, using a wooden spoon (picture A), until the mixture is pale, soft and fluffy. (This is called " creaming " the fat and sugar.)

5 Break the egg into a basin and whisk with a fork until frothy.

6 Add egg 2 tsps. at a time to creamed fat and sugar, beating well every time before adding any more (picture B).

7 Lightly fold in half the flour and coconut with a tablespoon (picture C). Add the remaining flour and coconut and stir this in; if necessary, add 2–3 tsps. milk or water to make the mixture soft enough to drop easily from the spoon when this is held above the bowl and shaken.

8 Place 1 heaped tsp. of mixture in each paper case, pushing it from spoon with knife (picture D). Smooth tops, then decorate top of each bun with a piece of cherry.

9 Bake towards the top of the oven for 15–20 minutes, until well-risen, golden and firm to the touch.

10 Remove from the oven and place on the cooling rack.

For a special occasion, bake the buns without the cherry decoration; when they are cool, make up some glacé icing (see page 142), using 50 g icing sugar. Put a little of the icing on each bun, sprinkle with desiccated coconut and top with half a glacé cherry, a chocolate drop or small sweet or a piece of crystallised angelica.

CHOCOLATE BUNS

Ingredients

50 g self-raising flour
25 g cocoa
50 g margarine
50 g caster sugar
1 egg
2–3 tsps. water to mix

For the Butter Cream
100 g icing sugar
50 g butter or margarine
1 tsp. vanilla essence, *or*
  2 level tsps. instant coffee

Utensils

10 paper baking cases
Baking tray
Sieve, plate
Mixing bowl
Wooden spoon, fork,
  teaspoon, tablespoon,
  vegetable knife
2 basins
Cooling rack

1 Heat the oven to 190°C. (375°F.), mark 5.

2 Place the paper cases evenly over the baking tray (not too near the edges).

3 Sift the flour and cocoa on to a plate.

4 Cream the margarine and sugar with a wooden spoon until the mixture is pale and fluffy.

5 Break the egg into a basin and whisk with a fork. Add the egg to the creamed fat and sugar 2 tsps. at a time, beating well each time.

6 Fold in half the flour and cocoa with a tablespoon, then add the remaining flour and cocoa and sufficient water to give a mixture soft enough to drop easily from the spoon when this is shaken.

7 Put a good tsp. of the mixture in each paper case and bake towards the top of the oven for 15–20 minutes, until the buns are well-risen and firm to the touch.

8 Remove the buns and place on the cooling rack. When they are cold, cut a round from the top of each with the pointed knife (picture A).

9 Meanwhile make the butter cream (picture B). Sift icing sugar into a basin, add butter or margarine and cream well until smooth and soft. If coffee is used, dissolve it in 1 tsp. water; now beat in the coffee or the vanilla essence.

10 Place 1 tsp. butter cream in each bun (picture C).

11 Replace tops (picture D); they can be cut in half, the pieces being pushed in at an angle to form " wings ".

VICTORIA SANDWICH CAKE

Ingredients
100 g self-raising flour
100 g butter or margarine
100 g caster sugar
2 eggs
1-2 rounded tbsps. jam
Caster sugar for top of
 cake

Utensils
Two 6-in (15 cm) cake tins
Greaseproof paper, pencil,
 scissors
Sieve, plate
Mixing bowl, basin
Wooden spoon, fork or
 whisk, tablespoon, tea-
 spoon, round-bladed knife
Cooling rack

1 Heat the oven to 190°C. (375°F.), mark 5.

2 Place one of the cake tins on a double sheet of grease-proof paper and draw round it (picture A); cut with the scissors just inside the pencil line to give two rounds of paper. Grease the sides and base of the two tins, put in the paper rounds and grease these also.

3 Sift the flour on to a plate.

4 Cream the fat and sugar, using a wooden spoon, until the mixture is pale, soft and fluffy.

5 Break the eggs into a basin and whisk with a fork.

6 Beat egg 2 tsps. at a time into creamed fat and sugar, making sure each addition is well mixed in before adding any more, or the mixture will " curdle "—lose its smooth, creamy appearance and become uneven and broken up.

7 Lightly stir in half the flour with a tablespoon, taking this round the outside of the mixture, then drawing it through the centre (picture B). This is known as " folding in " the flour. Fold in the rest of the flour.

8 Place half the mixture in each tin and level it with a knife (picture C).

9 Bake both cakes on the same shelf, just above the oven centre, for about 20 minutes, or until well-risen, golden and firm to the touch and beginning to shrink away from the side of the tin.

10 Turn the cakes out on to the cooling rack and remove the papers. When cool, sandwich together with the jam (picture D) and sprinkle the top with caster sugar.

Do you think that this cake is (*a*) nicer, (*b*) dearer than one made from a packet mix?

SYRUP FLAPJACKS

Ingredients	Utensils
100 g margarine	A small Yorkshire pudding
25 g granulated sugar	tin
2 level tbsps. golden syrup	Mixing bowl
200 g rolled oats	Wooden spoon, tablespoon,
¼ level tsp. salt	teaspoon, round-bladed
	knife
	Small saucepan

1 Heat the oven to 170°C. (325°F.), mark 3.

2 Grease the Yorkshire pudding tin.

3 Put the margarine and sugar into a mixing bowl and beat with a wooden spoon until pale, soft and fluffy.

4 Measure the syrup into a pan (dipping the tablespoon into very hot water before putting it into the syrup, so that the syrup does not stick); heat it gently.

5 Stir the warm syrup into the creamed fat and sugar mixture and work in the oats and salt until well blended.

6 Put mixture in tin, pressing down evenly (picture A).

7 Bake in centre of oven for 30–45 minutes till golden.

8 Cut into fingers (picture B) and leave in the tin until cold —if the pieces are removed whilst hot, they may crumble.

GINGER SNAPS

Ingredients	Utensils
50 g butter or margarine	2 baking trays
2 rounded tbsps. golden	Small saucepan
syrup	Tablespoon, teaspoon
25 g caster sugar	Sieve
100 g self-raising flour	Mixing bowl
2 level tsps. ground ginger	Palette knife
½ level tsp. bicarbonate of	
soda	

1 Heat the oven to 190°C. (375°F.), mark 5.

2 Grease the baking trays.

3 Melt the butter, syrup and sugar together.

4 Sift the flour, ginger and bicarbonate of soda into the bowl. Stir the syrup into them.

5 Pull off pieces of mixture, roll into small balls and drop them on to the baking sheets, leaving space for them to spread—you should have about 20 snaps.

6 Bake in the centre of the oven for 15 minutes.

7 Allow to cool slightly before lifting off the trays.

GINGERBREAD

Ingredients	Utensils
400 g plain flour	A 7-in (18 cm) square tin
1 level tsp. salt	Teaspoon, tablespoon,
1 level tbsp. ground ginger	fork, wooden spoon
1 level tbsp. baking powder	Sieve
1 level tsp. bicarbonate of	Mixing bowl
soda	Small pan
3 level tbsps. treacle	Small basin
3 level tbsps. syrup	Measuring jug
200 g brown sugar	Cooling rack
150 g butter or margarine	
1 egg	
250 ml milk	

1 Heat the oven to 180°C. (350°F.), mark 4.

2 Grease the cake tin and line with greaseproof paper.

3 Sift into a mixing bowl the flour, salt, ginger, baking powder and bicarbonate of soda.

4 Put the treacle and syrup into a small pan, dipping the tablespoon into very hot water before measuring each spoonful (picture A).

5 Add the sugar and butter and warm gently (picture B).

6 Break egg into basin and whisk lightly with a fork.

7 Add treacle mixture, egg and milk to flour mixture in bowl and mix well with a wooden spoon (picture C).

8 Pour into the prepared tin (picture D) and bake in the centre of the oven for about 1½ hours, or until firm to the touch. Cool on the rack. Cut up and, if you wish, decorate with small pieces of preserved ginger.

COBURG CAKES

Heat the oven to 180°C. (350°F.), mark 4. Grease 18 patty tins. Blanch and chop 50 g almonds and put some in each tin. Sift into a mixing bowl 200 g plain flour, ½ level tsp. ginger, ½ level tsp. ground cinnamon, ½ level tsp. mixed spice and 1 level tsp. bicarbonate of soda. Warm 1 tbsp. syrup, 100 g brown sugar and 100 g margarine gently. Add the syrup mixture to the flour mixture in the bowl and add also 1 beaten egg and 4 tbsps. milk; stir well. Divide the cake mixture equally between the tins and bake in the centre of the oven for 20 minutes.

BOSTON BROWNIES (American)

Ingredients	Utensils
75 g self-raising flour	Loaf tin 11 by 7 by 1½ in.
½ level tsp. salt	(28 by 18 by 4 cm)
75 g butter	Sieve, plate
50 g bitter chocolate	Teaspoon, tablespoon,
2 large eggs	wooden spoon, cook's knife
150 g caster sugar	Saucepan, basin
½ tsp. vanilla essence	Mixing bowl
50 g walnuts	Chopping board

1 Heat oven to 180°C. (350°F.), mark 4; grease loaf tin.

2 Sift the flour and salt on to a plate.

3 Boil a pan of water; place butter and chocolate in a basin and stand this over the water to melt (picture A).

4 Break the eggs into the bowl, add sugar and essence and mix well; gradually beat in the chocolate mixture (picture B).

5 Chop the walnuts and mix with the flour.

6 Using a tablespoon, stir the flour and walnuts into the egg mixture (picture C).

7 Pour into the prepared tin (picture D) and bake in the centre of the oven for 35–40 minutes, until cooked. Cool in the tin, then cut into 16 portions.

CRUNCHY DATE SQUARES (American)

For the Filling	*For the Crumble*
100 g cooking dates, chopped	75 g plain flour
25 g brown sugar	½ level tsp. bicarbonate of soda
125 ml water	50 g rolled oats
½ tsp. lemon essence	100 g soft brown sugar
	100 g margarine

Heat oven to 190°C. (375°F.), mark 5. Grease an 18 cm sandwich tin and line base with greaseproof paper. Simmer dates with 25 g sugar, water and lemon essence for 5 minutes.

Mix flour, bicarbonate of soda, rolled oats and 100 g sugar. Melt the margarine and stir it into the dry ingredients till the mixture sticks together. Press half this mixture into the tin, then pour the dates over. Cover with remaining crumble, pressing it well down. Bake at centre of oven for 30 minutes, until golden and firm. Serve cut into squares.

A

B

C

D

SWISS ROLL

Ingredients	Utensils
2 eggs	Swiss roll tin
50 g caster sugar	Greaseproof paper
50 g plain flour	Large saucepan, small pan,
1 tbsp. hot water	pan stand
Caster sugar to dredge	Basin, mixing bowl
paper	Whisk, sieve
4 tbsps. jam	Tablespoon, round-bladed
	knife, cook's knife
	Clean tea towel
	Cooling rack

1 Heat the oven to 220°C. (425°F.), mark 7.

2 Grease and line tin and thoroughly grease again.

3 Half-fill large pan with water and bring to the boil; put pan on table on the pan stand.

4 Crack eggs, put with 50 g sugar into mixing bowl and rest this on the saucepan. Whisk until mixture is really stiff, pale and fluffy. Remove bowl from pan and whisk for a further few minutes to cool the mixture.

5 Sift the flour into the mixture; using a tablespoon, fold it in very lightly until all is thoroughly mixed.

6 Add the water and mix in carefully with a metal spoon.

7 Pour mixture into tin, spreading out evenly with knife.

8 Bake just above centre of oven for 7–9 minutes—the sponge is cooked when it is golden-brown and feels spongy.

9 Warm the jam gently in the small pan.

10 Wring tea towel out in water, spread on table, cover with greaseproof paper and sprinkle with remaining sugar.

11 Take cake from oven and turn out at once on to the sugared paper. Using the cook's knife, trim edges off the 2 long sides and the farther short side (see picture A).

12 Quickly spread the melted jam evenly on the cake to within 3 cm of the cut short edge.

13 Make a cut half-way through the sponge right across the cake, 3 cm from the untrimmed end (picture B).

14 Turn untrimmed end over, press down firmly, then roll sponge by pulling near end of paper over cake and away from yourself (picture C); roll the cake firmly.

15 Leave for 5 minutes (picture D), then unwrap and put on cooling rack. Dredge with sugar before serving.

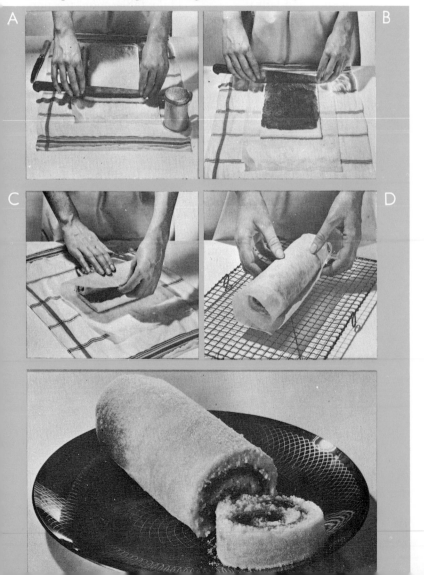

NUT ROCKS

Ingredients

75 g shelled almonds or
   walnuts
110 g icing sugar
2 egg whites (quite free
   of shell and yolk)
1 tsp. almond or vanilla
   essence

Utensils

Baking tray
Large saucepan
Chopping board
Cook's knife, round-bladed
   knife, tablespoon, teaspoon
Sieve, mixing bowl, basin
Whisk

1 Heat the oven to 150°C. (300°F.), mark 2.

2 Grease and flour the baking tray.

3 Half-fill saucepan with water and bring to boil.

4 Chop the nuts on the board.

5 Sift the icing sugar into the mixing bowl.

6 Add egg white, stand bowl over pan of hot water and whisk till mixture clings stiffly to whisk (picture A).

7 Add nuts and flavouring to mixture and mix well.

8 Pile in teaspoonfuls on the baking tray (picture B).

9 Bake in the centre of the oven until crisp on the outside and creamy in colour—about 20–30 minutes.

Notes:

1 This amount makes 10–12 nut rocks.

2 See page 16 for method of separating eggs. Use the yolks in an omelette, scrambled eggs or egg custard tart.

MERINGUES

Ingredients

Olive or salad oil
2 egg whites
100 g caster sugar

Utensils

Baking tray
Silicone or greaseproof
   paper
Mixing bowl
Whisk, tablespoon

1 Heat the oven to 140°C. (275°F.), mark ½.

2 Line the baking tray with silicone or greaseproof paper (very lightly brushed with oil).

3 Whisk egg whites in bowl until they stand up in stiff peaks.

4 Sprinkle half the sugar over the whites and whisk until the mixture is stiff again.

5 Fold in the remaining sugar with a tablespoon.

6 Pile in spoonfuls on the tray.

7 Put in centre of oven until quite dry and crisp, but still white—about 2½–3 hours. If necessary, open oven door slightly to prevent the meringues from browning.

CAKE DECORATING

To Prepare the Cake and Decorations

1 Make a Victoria sandwich or sponge cake and fill the centre with jam, whipped cream or butter cream (see below).

2 Make sure the cake has a flat top if it is to be iced—if necessary, turn it upside-down and use the underside.

3 Brush away any crumbs or loose bits which would stick in the icing and spoil the effect. If the sides are to be decorated, do this next (see page 142).

4 Place the cake on a cooling tray so that it is easy to move when finished—the icing on a newly decorated cake might crack if you moved it from one plate to another.

5 Prepare the decorations as required, e.g., chop walnuts, flake almonds; cut glacé cherries or angelica into small pieces; cut crystallised orange or lemon into triangles; slice crystallised ginger; grate chocolate. Other favourite decorations are desiccated coconut; chocolate drops, vermicelli or shot; silver or coloured balls; little sweets such as dragees and jelly babies (especially liked by small children); candles (for birthday cakes).

BUTTER CREAM

Ingredients	Utensils
100 g icing sugar	Sieve, basin
50 g butter or margarine	Knife, wooden spoon,
A little milk if necessary	teaspoon
Flavouring	

Sift the icing sugar into a basin and add the butter or margarine, cut into small pieces. Cream them together with a wooden spoon until pale, smooth and creamy, adding 1–2 tsps. milk if necessary. Flavour by beating in any of the following: A few drops of vanilla essence; 1 level tbsp. sifted cocoa or 25 g melted and cooled chocolate; 2 level tsps. instant coffee powder dissolved in 1 tsp. water; the finely grated rind of 1 orange or lemon; 50 g chopped walnuts or preserved ginger.

To Use as a Filling: Spread the butter cream evenly over the lower half of the cake with a round-bladed knife, taking it right to the edges, then put the top half of the cake in place (see top picture).

To Use as a Topping: Pile the butter cream on top of the cake, spread it out smoothly and evenly to the edges until it completely covers the surface. A pattern can then be marked with a fork or skewer and decorations can be added—see bottom picture.

A

B

CAKE DECORATING (Continued)

GLACÉ ICING

Ingredients	Utensils
200 g icing sugar	Sieve, basin, saucepan
Water to mix	Wooden spoon, teaspoon

Sift sugar into a basin. Warm some water gently in the pan and add it to the sugar 1 tsp. at a time, stirring until all the sugar is mixed in and an icing is obtained which is thick enough to coat the back of the spoon when this is dipped in the mixture and held above the bowl.

This basic glacé icing may be varied as follows:

Coffee: Add 2 tsps. instant coffee dissolved in 1 tsp. of the water.

Chocolate: Add 1 level tbsp. cocoa when sifting the sugar.

Orange or Lemon: Squeeze the juice from an orange or lemon and use this instead of water to mix the icing.

Coloured Icings: For these you need bottled food colourings. Dip a skewer into the bottle, then shake off a few drops of colouring into plain icing and mix until well blended. Go very carefully, as you need only a very small amount of colouring to give a really strong colour.

DECORATING THE SIDES OF THE CAKE

Any cake can be decorated round the sides. Do this before the top is decorated, to avoid accidentally disturbing it.

With Jam, Coconut, Nuts, etc.: Sieve 4 tbsps. apricot or raspberry jam into a basin and brush round sides of prepared cake, or spread with a knife. Put some desiccated coconut on greaseproof paper. Holding the cake on its side, roll it in the coconut until an even layer sticks to the jam and the sides are completely coated (picture A).
The coconut may be replaced by finely chopped walnuts or flaked almonds.

With Butter Cream: Instead of jam, use butter cream (made with 100 g icing sugar and 50 g butter). Chopped nuts, crushed biscuit or cake crumbs or chocolate vermicelli can then be used to coat the sides of the cake.

ICING THE CAKE

1 Prepare the cake, the decorations and icing as already described and have ready a round-bladed knife.

2 Pour the icing on to the centre top of the cake (picture B). Using the knife and working quickly, spread it evenly to the edges of the cake; stop just inside the edges, to prevent any icing dropping down the sides.

3 Quickly put any decorations in place before the icing hardens, so that when it is set they will be firmly held.

DATE LOAF

Ingredients

150 g dates
50 g nuts
200 g plain flour
100 g margarine
100 g sugar
50 g raisins, stoned or
  seedless
1 level tsp. baking powder
1 level tsp. bicarbonate
  of soda
125 ml milk

Utensils

Loaf tin 3½ by 7½ inches
  (9 by 19 cm)
Cook's knife, tablespoon,
  teaspoon
Chopping board
Sieve, mixing bowl
Plate
Small basin

1 Heat the oven to 180°C. (350°F.), mark 4. Grease the loaf tin.

2 Chop the dates and nuts.

3 Sift the flour into the mixing bowl.

4 Cut the margarine into small pieces on a plate, add to the mixing bowl and rub it in, using your finger-tips, until the mixture is free from lumps and looks like fine breadcrumbs.

5 Add the sugar, chopped dates, nuts and raisins.

6 Dissolve the baking powder and bicarbonate of soda in the milk. Stirring with the tablespoon, mix with the dry ingredients (picture A); add a little more milk if necessary, so that the mixture will drop from the spoon when this is held over the bowl.

7 Put into the loaf tin (picture B) and bake in the centre of the oven for 1 hour. Serve sliced.

A

B

A family high tea usually consists of a simple main course followed by a sweet, or bread, butter and jam and a selection of cakes. The main course should include a protein food such as meat, fish, eggs, cheese. Sausage Flan, Scotch Eggs and Beef Pasties are examples of popular lighter main courses. Include fresh vegetables or salad.

EGGS MORNAY

Ingredients	Utensils
4 eggs	Chopping board
25 g butter	A shallow ovenproof dish
25 g flour	Saucepan
250 ml milk	Tablespoon, wooden spoon,
50 g cheese, grated	cook's knife
Salt and pepper	Grater, plate
Butter for topping	
Chopped parsley for garnish	

1 Put the eggs on to hard-boil for 12 mins. Remove from heat, plunge into cold water and remove shells.

2 Melt the butter, stir in the flour and cook the mixture for 2–3 mins. Remove from the heat.

3 Gradually add the milk, stirring all the time. Bring to the boil and continue to stir until the mixture is thick; adjust the seasoning.

4 Add most of the cheese, saving a little for garnishing.

5 Slice the eggs; lay them in the dish.

6 Pour sauce over eggs, sprinkle with remaining cheese, dot with butter and pop the dish under a medium grill until cheese is melted and golden brown.

7 Garnish with parsley.

WELSH RAREBIT

Ingredients	Utensils
200 g Cheddar, Lancashire or Cheshire cheese	Grater, plate
	Grillpan
4 thick slices of bread	Round-bladed knife, table-
Butter	spoon, teaspoon, wooden
$\frac{1}{2}$-1 level tsp. dry mustard	spoon
Salt and pepper	Large serving plate
A little milk	Saucepan (heavy-based if possible)

1 Grate cheese on to plate, using large holes of grater.

2 Toast the bread on both sides, butter and keep warm on a large serving plate under a very low grill.

3 Put the cheese in a saucepan and heat very gently until it melts, stirring all the time.

4 Add mustard, a good sprinkling of salt and pepper and enough milk to make a soft, creamy mixture (picture A).

5 Stir well and pour over the toast; increase the heat of the grill, put the toast underneath and cook for a few minutes, until golden and bubbling. Serve at once.

Note: Although we suggest using milk to mix, beer is traditionally used in making Welsh rarebit.

SAVOURY CHEESE TOAST

Ingredients	Utensils
200 g Cheddar, Lancashire or Cheshire cheese	Grater, plate
	Grillpan
4 thick slices of bread	Round-bladed knife, tea-
Butter	spoon, tablespoon
$\frac{1}{2}$ level tsp. dry mustard *or* a few drops of Worcestershire sauce; salt and pepper	Large serving plate
	Basin
A little milk to mix	

1 Grate cheese on to plate, using large holes of grater.

2 Toast the bread, butter it and keep warm on a large serving plate under the grill, turning this very low.

3 Put the cheese in a basin, add seasonings and stir in enough milk to make a spreadable mixture (picture B). Turn up grill.

4 Pile on toast, taking it right to the edges.

5 Put the toast back under a hot grill and cook for a few minutes, until golden and bubbly.

Can you name 6 other cheeses and do you know which part of the world they come from? Find out the difference between processed cheese and ordinary cheese.

A

B

CHEESE AND ONION PIE

Ingredients	Utensils
150 g plain flour	Sieve, mixing bowl
$\frac{1}{2}$ level tsp. salt	Teaspoon, tablespoon,
80 g lard (*or*	round-bladed knife, cook's
40 g lard and 40 g	knife, fork, skewer
margarine)	Plate, 2 basins
Cold water to mix	Chopping board
2 large onions	Saucepan
Salt and pepper	Grater
200 g Cheddar cheese	Pastry board, dredger,
1 egg	rolling pin, pastry brush
A little milk to glaze	A 7-in (18 cm) pie plate
pastry	Baking tray

1 Heat the oven to 200°C. (400°F.), mark 6.

2 Sift the flour and salt into a mixing bowl. Cut the fat into small pieces and rub it into the flour, using the fingertips, until no lumps remain and the mixture looks like fine breadcrumbs.

3 Add the water 2 tsps. at a time, stirring until the mixture begins to stick together. Using one hand, collect it together and knead into a firm, smooth dough.

4 Skin and chop onions, put into saucepan, cover with cold water, add $\frac{1}{2}$ level tsp. salt and simmer for 10 minutes.

5 Using the largest holes of the grater, grate the cheese on to a plate. When the onions are cooked, drain off the water by tipping the contents of the pan into the sieve or a colander over a basin.

6 Break the egg into a basin and whisk with a fork; add the onion, cheese and some salt and pepper.

7 Halve pastry and roll one piece on a floured board into a round a little bigger than the pie plate. Line plate with pastry, taking care not to stretch it (picture A). Fill centre with cheese mixture.

8 Roll out remaining pastry to fit top of dish and place in position, damping the edges of the pastry before pressing them together. Trim the edges.

9 Hold down the edge of the pastry with the back of the first finger and make close horizontal cuts round the edge (picture B), then, using back of the knife blade, pull the edge of the pastry up at 3 cm intervals to form scallops. Brush the top of the pie with milk.

10 Place the pie on a baking tray and cook near the top of the oven for about 30 minutes, or until the pastry is golden.

A  B

BACON AND EGG PIE

Ingredients	Utensils
150 g plain flour	Sieve, mixing bowl
$\frac{1}{2}$ level tsp. salt	Round-bladed knife,
80 g lard (*or* 40 g lard	teaspoon, tablespoon,
and 40 g margarine)	cook's knife, fork
Cold water to mix	Plate, basin
150 g streaky bacon	Chopping board
2 eggs	Pastry board, dredger,
2 tbsps. milk	rolling pin, pastry brush
Salt and pepper	A 7-in (18 cm) pie plate
Extra milk to glaze the	Baking tray
pastry	

1 Heat the oven to 200°C. (400°F.), mark 6.

2 Sift the flour and salt into a mixing bowl, cut the fat into small pieces and rub into the flour, using the fingertips, until no lumps remain and the mixture looks like fine breadcrumbs.

3 Add the water 2 tsps. at a time, stirring with a round-bladed knife, until the mixture begins to stick together. Using one hand, collect the mixture together and knead into a firm dough.

4 Remove the rind from the bacon with a cook's knife and chop the rashers into 3 cm strips. Break the eggs into a basin (picture A), whisk lightly with a fork, then stir in the milk and some salt and pepper.

5 Divide the pastry evenly into 2 pieces and roll out one piece on a floured board into a round a little bigger than the pie plate. Line the plate with this pastry, taking care not to stretch it.

6 Put the chopped bacon in the pie and pour the egg mixture over (picture B).

7 Roll out the remaining pastry to fit the top of the plate and place it in position, damping the edges of the pastry before pressing them together (picture C). Trim the edges.

8 Make close horizontal cuts round the edge of the pie (see p. 137), then, using the back of the knife blade, pull up the edge of the pastry at 3 cm intervals, to form scallops. Brush the top of the pie with milk (picture D).

9 Place the pie on a baking tray and bake towards the top of the oven for about 30 minutes.

A

B

C

D

MACARONI CHEESE

Ingredients	Utensils
Salt, pepper, mustard	An ovenproof dish
100 g macaroni	Large saucepan, small sauce-
150 g cheese	pan, pan stand
40 g margarine	Teaspoon, tablespoon,
40 g flour	wooden spoon, skewer,
500 ml milk	cook's knife
1 tomato	Grater, plate
	Colander or sieve

1 Grease the ovenproof dish.

2 Half-fill the large saucepan with water and bring to the boil. Add 2 tsps. salt and drop in the macaroni; cook rapidly until tender—about 20 minutes.

3 Grate the cheese on to a plate.

4 Melt the margarine in the small saucepan and remove it from the heat. Add the flour (picture A), stir it in well with a wooden spoon, return the pan to the heat and cook until the mixture bubbles, then again remove from the heat.

5 Add the milk a little at a time, stirring thoroughly before adding any more (picture B),

6 Return the pan to the heat and bring to the boil, stirring all the time, until the sauce thickens (picture C).

7 Remove from the heat and add the cheese (saving 2 tbsps. for the top), with salt, pepper and mustard to taste.

8 Test the macaroni by prodding with a skewer—if it feels tender, pour it into the colander or sieve to drain. Add to the hot sauce and mix thoroughly (picture D); put into the dish and sprinkle top with remaining cheese.

9 Slice tomato and arrange down centre of dish.

10 Put the dish into a grill pan and place under a hot grill until the cheese is golden.

What kind of cheese would you use for cooking?

If you want to make macaroni cheese a little more exciting, add something extra to the sauce, such as 50 g chopped ham, 3 eggs, hard-boiled and sliced, or a packet of frozen vegetables, cooked as directed on the packet.

The cheese sauce can also be poured over a hot cooked vegetable such as cauliflower or leeks; finish as above.

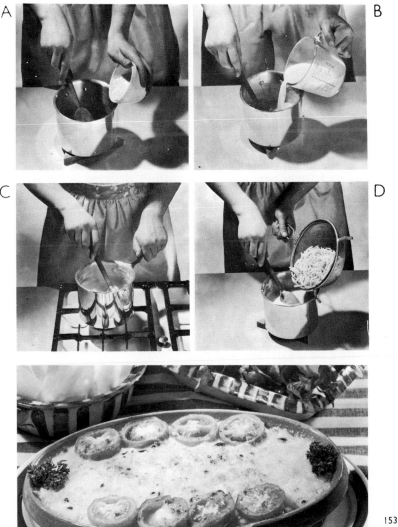

OMELETTES

Ingredients	Utensils
2 eggs	Small frying pan
Salt and pepper	Kitchen paper, dry cloth
15 g butter	Fork, tablespoon, palette knife, basin, serving plate

1 To prepare the pan, place over a gentle heat, sprinkle with salt and rub vigorously with kitchen paper. Tip out any loose salt, then rub pan with a clean, dry cloth. (Ideally, a special pan should be kept for omelettes.)

2 Break eggs into basin and whisk lightly with fork till yolks and whites are well mixed. Add 2 tbsps. water, salt and pepper, then mix well. Put serving plate to warm.

3 Melt butter in pan over medium heat, tilting pan so that whole surface is evenly greased (picture A).

4 Pour in egg mixture; holding fork with back of prongs flat on base of pan, gently stir mixture, drawing in the sides to the centre, so that the liquid egg can flow to the sides and cook (picture B).

5 Immediately the egg begins to set, stop stirring and leave pan over medium heat for a minute, until omelette is set and underside is lightly browned (picture C).

6 Using a palette knife, fold omelette, flicking one-third over to centre, then folding opposite side to centre (picture D).

7 Turn it out on to a hot plate, folded sides underneath.

Note: Don't cook an omelette too long, as this makes it too brown on the outside and rather tough.

Variations

CHEESE Grate 40 g cheese and mix 25 g of it with the eggs before cooking; sprinkle the rest over the top of the omelette after it has been folded.

MUSHROOM Wash and slice 50 g mushrooms and cook in small pan in a little butter until tender. Put them in the centre of the omelette before folding.

TOMATO Peel and roughly chop a large tomato. Put it in the centre of the omelette before folding.

BACON Rind and chop 2 rashers of bacon and fry in a small pan. Put in centre of omelette before folding.

SWEET Omit the salt and pepper. Spread with hot jam, marmalade or syrup before folding and sprinkle with sugar.

A

B

C

D

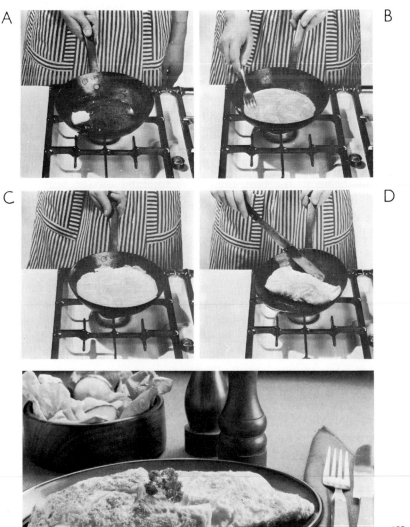

KEDGEREE

Ingredients

100 g rice
Salt and pepper
200 g smoked haddock
2 eggs
Parsley
50 g margarine

Utensils

2 large saucepans and 1 lid;
  1 small saucepan
Sieve
Chopping board
Teaspoon, tablespoon,
  cook's knife, fork
Plate, greaseproof paper
Serving dish

1 Bring a large pan of water to the boil.

2 Put the rice in a sieve and wash it under the cold tap.

3 Add 2 level tsps. salt and the rice to the boiling water and cook for 15 minutes, or until the rice is soft, boiling fast all the time.

4 Place the fish in a saucepan, cover with water, put on the lid, bring to the boil, then leave to stand off the heat for 5–10 minutes.

5 Put the eggs in a small pan of water, bring to the boil and allow to boil for 10 minutes.

6 Chop the parsley on a board to make about 2 level tsps. for garnish (picture A).

7 Drain the fish well, place on a board, remove the skin and bones and flake with a fork (picture B).

8 When the rice has cooked, turn it into the sieve and pour hot water through to separate the grains. Place on a plate, cover with greaseproof paper (picture C) and leave to dry for a few minutes in a warm place.

9 When the eggs have boiled for 10 minutes, plunge them into cold water; when they are cool, shell and then chop roughly.

10 Melt the margarine in a pan and add the rice, fish, egg and some salt and pepper. Stir thoroughly over a moderate heat until really hot (picture D).

11 Pile on a hot dish and garnish with chopped parsley.

SAVOURY RICE Cook 150 g rice as above. Meanwhile melt 50 g margarine in a pan and fry 1 finely chopped onion and 50 g chopped bacon until almost cooked. Add 4 skinned and chopped tomatoes and fry for 1 minute longer. Stir into the drained rice and serve in a hot dish, garnished with chopped parsley.

A

B

C

D

FISH CAKES

Ingredients	Utensils
350 g potatoes	Cook's knife, teaspoon,
Salt and pepper	tablespoon, round-bladed
200 g haddock fillet	knife, fork or masher,
A small bunch of parsley	fish slice
25 g butter	2 saucepans and lids
1 egg	Strainer
Dried breadcrumbs	2 plates, mixing bowl
Lard or cooking oil	Chopping board
A 3 cm cube of stale	Pastry board, dredger,
bread, free of crusts	pastry brush
	Greaseproof paper, kitchen
	paper
	Frying pan

1 Peel the potatoes and cut into even-sized pieces. Place in a saucepan, cover with cold water, add 1 tsp. salt, put on the lid, bring to the boil and leave to simmer for 20–30 minutes, or until soft.

2 Wash the haddock, place in another saucepan and cover with cold water. Put the lid on the pan, bring slowly to the boil, then turn off the heat and leave covered for 5 minutes, by which time the fish should be cooked.

3 Drain the fish well, turn it on to a plate, remove the skin and any bones and chop the fish roughly.

4 Wash parsley, remove large stalks and chop leaves finely with a cook's knife on a chopping board.

5 When potatoes are soft, drain well, place in mixing bowl and mash with a fork or masher until smooth. Add butter, salt, pepper, fish and parsley and mix well.

6 Turn mixture on to floured board and form into a roll with your hands. Cut into 8 slices (picture A) and shape evenly into cakes, using a round-bladed knife.

7 Break egg on to plate and whisk lightly. Place crumbs on greaseproof paper. Dip fish cakes in egg, brushing well, then remove with palette knife and place in crumbs (picture B). Coat well, patting crumbs into the surface with your hands, then knock off any loose ones.

8 Heat about 100 grams of lard or cooking oil in the frying pan. Drop the cube of bread into the hot fat; if it browns in 40–50 seconds, the fat is hot enough.

9 Add fish cakes about 4 at a time (over-crowding the pan makes the food break up when you turn it over). Fry till golden on underside, then turn them over with fish slice and fry on other side. When fish cakes are cooked, place on crumpled kitchen paper to absorb fat before serving.

A

B

POTATO CHEESE PIE

Ingredients	Utensils
450 g potatoes	Large saucepan
50 g cheese	Potato peeler or vegetable
2-3 tbsps. milk	knife, round-bladed knife,
Salt and pepper	fork, tablespoon, wooden
Parsley	spoon
	Pie dish
	Grater, plate

1 Peel the potatoes and cook in boiling salted water for about 20 minutes. Drain the water off (picture A) and mash the potatoes with a fork until smooth.

2 Grease the pie dish.

3 Grate cheese, using grater over plate (picture B).

4 Add milk, cheese, salt and pepper to the mashed potatoes in the pan (picture C) and warm gently, beating with the wooden spoon until creamy and warmed through.

5 Turn the mixture into the greased pie dish, spread it evenly and draw a fork across the top to decorate it (picture D).

6 Put under a hot grill until the top is golden-brown.

7 Garnish with a sprig of parsley and serve hot.

POTATO AND ONION PIE

Slice an onion and fry it until golden in a little fat. Make creamed potatoes as above, put half the mixture in the dish, spread the fried onion on top and then cover with the remaining potato. Slice a tomato and arrange as a decoration on the pie. Finish as above.

CHEESY POTATOES Choose 4 large potatoes, scrub them well and make a cut in the skins lengthwise all the way round. Bake near the top of a 200°C. (400°F.), mark 6 oven for 1-1½ hours, until they feel soft. Cut them in half through the scored mark, then, using a teaspoon, scoop out all the cooked potato. Put it into a basin, mash with a fork, add

25 g butter, salt, pepper and 150 g grated cheese and beat with a wooden spoon until creamy. Pile back into the skins, sprinkle on more grated cheese and brown under a hot grill.

EGGS IN NESTS Make a hollow in each Cheesy Potato and crack an egg into this " nest ". Sprinkle with grated cheese, salt and pepper and brown under the grill until the egg is set.

SCOTCH EGGS

Ingredients

5 eggs

200 g sausage-meat or sausages

Lard or cooking oil

A little flour

$\frac{1}{2}$ pkt. browned bread-crumbs

A 3 cm cube of stale bread, free of crusts

Utensils

Small saucepan

Vegetable knife, fork

Chopping board

Basin

Deep-fat frying pan and basket

Plate, pastry brush

Greaseproof paper, kitchen paper

1 Put 4 of the eggs into a small pan of water, bring to the boil and allow to boil for 10 minutes.

2 Divide the sausage-meat into 4 equal-sized rounds. (If sausages are used, remove the meat from the skins.) Flatten each piece to about 1 cm thick.

3 When the eggs have cooked for 10 minutes, plunge them into cold water and shell when cool.

4 Put enough lard or cooking oil in the deep-fat fryer to half-fill it.

5 Dust the shelled eggs with flour.

6 Cover each egg with sausage-meat, doing this as evenly as possible, to give a good shape (picture A); avoid cracks, which would open up during the cooking.

7 Break the remaining egg on to the plate and whisk lightly with a fork.

8 Put the crumbs on a large piece of greaseproof paper.

9 Brush the Scotch eggs well with beaten egg (picture B) then put them in the crumbs and coat well, patting the crumbs into the surface with your hands and knocking off any loose ones.

10 Drop the cube of bread into the hot fat; if it browns in 60 seconds, the fat is hot enough.

11 Place the eggs in the frying basket and lower gently into the fat (picture C). Fry for 8–10 minutes, until the eggs are golden-brown.

12 Remove them from the fat and drain on crumpled kitchen paper (picture D).

13 To serve, cut the eggs in half lengthwise and serve with salad.

Do you prefer to use lard or cooking oil for frying?

A

B

C

D

CHEESE AND CHUTNEY PIE

Ingredients

1 pkt. (212 g) frozen
  puff pastry
150 g Cheddar cheese
2 eggs
2 level tbsps. cornflour
250 ml milk
Salt and pepper
2 level tbsps. chutney

Utensils

Grater, plate, 3 basins
Wooden spoon, tablespoon,
  round-bladed knife, whisk
  or fork
Measuring jug, saucepan
Pastry board, dredger,
  rolling pin, pastry brush
A 7-in (18 cm) pie plate
Baking tray

1 Heat the oven to 220°C. (425°F.), mark 7.

2 Thaw pastry at room temperature.

3 Using the large holes of the grater, grate the cheese on to a plate. Separate the eggs, placing the yolks in one basin and the whites in another.

4 Using a wooden spoon, blend the cornflour with 2 tbsps. of the milk in a basin. Heat the rest of the milk in a saucepan and when it boils, pour it on to the cornflour, stirring all the time.

5 Return mixture to pan and bring slowly to boil again, stirring all the time until sauce thickens. Remove from heat and stir in cheese (picture A), egg yolks (retaining just a little) and some salt and pepper.

6 Divide pastry into 2 pieces and shape each into a round with the hands; put one piece on a floured board and roll out into a round a little bigger than pie plate. Line plate, taking care not to stretch pastry.

7 Spread chutney over bottom of pie. Whisk egg whites until they are stiff and fluffy (picture B), stir gently into cheese sauce and pour mixture over chutney.

8 Roll out remaining pastry to fit top of dish and put in place, damping edges before pressing together. Trim edges.

9 Hold down edge of pastry with back of first finger and make close horizontal cuts round edge of pie, then, using the back of the knife blade, pull up edge of pastry at 3 cm intervals to form scallops.

10 Brush the top of the pastry with the remaining egg yolk (diluted with a little water). Place the pie on a baking tray and cook towards the top of the oven for about 25–30 minutes, until well risen and golden.

The chutney in the filling can be replaced by chopped and fried onion, tomato or bacon.
Serve Cheese and Chutney Pie either hot or cold. A cold pie would be ideal to take on a picnic. Have some lettuce or small tomatoes to eat with it.

A

B

SAUSAGE FLAN

Ingredients
100 g plain flour
A pinch of salt
50 g lard (*or* 25 g lard
and 25 g margarine)
Water to mix
1 onion
4 streaky bacon rashers
15 g lard for frying
1 egg
300 g sausage-meat
1 level tsp. mixed herbs
Salt and pepper
1 tomato (optional)

Utensils
Sieve, mixing bowl
Round-bladed knife, tea-
spoon, cook's knife, fork
Plate, 2 basins
Pastry board, dredger,
rolling pin, pastry brush
A 7-in (18 cm) pie plate or
sandwich cake tin
Chopping board
Frying pan

1 Heat the oven to 200°C. (400°F.), mark 6.

2 Sift the flour and salt into the mixing bowl. Cut the fat into small pieces and rub it into the flour until the mixture looks like fine breadcrumbs.

3 Add water 2 tsps. at a time, stirring with a round-bladed knife till mixture sticks together. Using one hand, collect together to give a firm dough and knead lightly.

4 Turn the pastry on to a floured board and shape into a round with your hands. Roll out 3 cm larger all round than the plate or tin. Line the plate with it, taking care not to stretch the pastry.

5 Using the round-bladed knife, trim off any extra pastry. Damp the edges and fold under 1 cm all the way round; crimp the edges, using your fingers.

6 Peel the onion and chop finely with a cook's knife on a chopping board. Remove the bacon rinds and chop the rashers into 1 cm strips.

7 Melt 15 g lard in the frying pan and fry onion and bacon till golden. Remove from pan, draining well.

8 Break egg into a basin and whisk lightly with fork. Mix sausage-meat, onion and bacon, herbs, salt and pepper; add egg and beat well with a fork (picture A).

9 Spread this mixture over pastry case (picture B). Bake towards top of oven for 15 minutes, or till pastry is set. Turn down oven to 180°C. (350°F.), mark 4 and cook for a further 25 minutes, or until sausage-meat is cooked.

Decoration (Optional): Slice tomato thinly, halve each slice and put a border of these half-slices round edge of pie when oven heat is turned down, i.e., after 15 minutes.

A

B

BEEF PASTIES

Ingredients

For the Pastry
200 g plain flour
A pinch of salt
100 g lard (*or* 50 g lard
  and 50 g margarine)
Water to mix
A little milk to glaze

For the Filling
1 onion
1 potato
1 tomato
200 g minced beef
Salt and pepper

Utensils

Sieve, mixing bowl
Round-bladed knife, tea-
  spoon, tablespoon,
  vegetable knife, fork
Plate, basin
Chopping board
Pastry board, dredger,
  rolling pin, pastry brush
Small saucepan lid
Baking tray

1 Heat the oven to 220°C. (425°F.), mark 7.

2 Sift the flour and salt into a mixing bowl. Cut the fat into small pieces and rub it into the flour until the mixture looks like fine breadcrumbs.

3 Add water 2 tsps. at a time, stirring with the knife until the mixture sticks together. Using one hand, collect it together to give a firm dough and knead lightly.

4 Peel the onion, potato and tomato. Chop the onion and tomato and dice the potato. Using a fork, mix the meat, vegetables, salt and pepper in a basin until well blended.

5 Roll out the pastry on a floured board and cut into 4 rounds, using a small saucepan lid as cutter (picture A). Place a quarter of the meat mixture in the centre of each round of pastry.

6 Wet the edges of the pastry, draw them up and press firmly together over the top of the pastry. Crimp the edges with your fingers (picture B) and brush the pastry with milk.

7 Place on a baking tray and cook towards the top of the oven for about 15 minutes, or until the pastry begins to brown, then lower the heat to 170°C. (325°F.), mark 3 and bake for another 45–60 minutes, depending on the size of the pasties.

BACON PASTIES

1 onion	½ level tsp. mixed herbs
4 tomatoes	Salt and pepper
150 g bacon, rinded	

Peel the onion and tomatoes and chop them. Chop the bacon and mix with the other ingredients in a basin. Use as a filling for pasties made as above.

A   B

BREAD BAPS

Ingredients	Utensils
125 ml milk and water	Measuring jug
1 level tsp. sugar	Small pan
2 level tsps. dried yeast	Teaspoon, wooden spoon, fork
200 g plain flour	
1 level tsp. salt	Sieve, mixing bowl
25 g margarine or lard	Pastry board, dredger
	Tea towel, foil or polythene bag
	Baking tray, pastry brush

1 Pour the milk and water into the pan and warm very slightly, so that it feels just warm to your little finger (picture A).

2 Stir in the sugar. Sprinkle the dried yeast on top of the liquid (picture B) and leave in a warm place for 10 minutes, or until it is frothy, which shows that the yeast is " activated ".

3 Sift the flour and salt into the bowl and rub in the fat.

4 Make a hole in the centre of the dry ingredients and pour in the liquid; using a wooden spoon, gradually stir in the flour to make a firm dough (picture C). Beat until it will leave the sides of the bowl cleanly.

5 Turn the dough on to a lightly floured board and knead for 10–15 minutes by folding the dough towards you (picture D), then pushing down and away from you with the heel of the hand. Give the dough a quarter-turn and repeat the kneading, developing a rocking rhythm. This pulling and stretching of the dough ensures an even texture and a good volume in the finished loaf.

6 Sprinkle some extra flour in the mixing bowl, put in the dough (picture E) and cover with a damp tea towel or foil or place the bowl and dough in a polythene bag to keep the dough moist and prevent " skinning ".

7 Leave dough to rise until it doubles in size and will spring back when pressed with a floured finger (picture F). Rising time varies with the temperature, so arrange process to suit your convenience. If dough is just left at room temperature, allow about 2 hours; if it is put in a warm place, allow 1 hour. (*Continued on page 172*)

BREAD BAPS (Continued)

8 Heat the oven to 220°C. (425°F.), mark 7. Grease a baking tray.

9 When the dough is risen, turn it on to a floured board and knead again for 2–3 minutes, to get rid of any large holes (picture A).

10 When the dough is smooth, divide it in half (picture B); shape each into a round and place on the baking tray. Prick all over the top with a fork.

11 Cover the dough with a damp tea towel or put in a polythene bag and leave for about 20 minutes until twice the size. (This is called proving.)

12 For a crisp crust, brush the dough over with very salty water—for a floury finish, brush it with milk and water and sprinkle with flour (picture C).

13 Bake in the centre of the oven for 30 minutes, or until the crust is a deep golden shade (picture D); when the loaves are tapped underneath with the knuckles, they should sound hollow.

FRUIT BAPS Work into the dough 50 g currants, 50 g sultanas and 25 g sugar; knead well before shaping.

POPPY SEED LOAF Shape dough into a long, thin loaf and cut crosswise slits down its length. After proving, brush it with beaten egg and sprinkle with poppy seeds.

BOAT LOAF Cut off a small piece of the dough. Shape the larger piece into a fairly fat but tapering oval. Roll out the small piece in your hands till long enough to put along middle of loaf; tuck both ends underneath.

BREAD FLOUR Bakers use what is called " strong " flour when making bread, not the " soft " type that is sold for home baking. " Strong " flour gives a dough that is more elastic and so is easier to knead and produces loaves of a better shape and texture. If there is a baker in your area who still does his own baking, he may sell you some of this special flour; some grocers also stock it.

FRESH YEAST When using fresh yeast, omit stage 2 and do not add the sugar or yeast to the warmed liquid, but rub it into the flour, salt and fat mixture. Stir in the sugar and continue from stage 4 as above.

ROLLS

Ingredients

150 ml milk
1 level tsp. sugar
2 level tsps. dried yeast
200 g plain flour
1 level tsp. salt
25 g margarine or lard

Utensils

Measuring jug, small pan
Teaspoon, knife, wooden
 spoon, fork
Sieve, mixing bowl
Tea towel, foil or polythene
 bag to cover bowl
Pastry board, dredger, pastry
 brush, baking tray

1 Slightly warm milk in pan until it feels just warm to your little finger. Stir in sugar. Sprinkle the dried yeast on the top of the milk, beat lightly with a fork and leave in a warm place for 10–15 minutes, until frothy.

2 Rub fat into flour. Make a hole in centre of dry ingredients and pour in liquid. Using a wooden spoon, gradually stir in flour to make a soft dough, then beat well till smooth and elastic.

3 Cover and allow to rise till it is twice its size.

4 When the dough is risen, turn it on to a floured board and knead for a few minutes. Divide into 12 pieces, knead each lightly and shape as desired—for example:

Plait: Divide dough into 3, shape each into a long roll and plait, joining the ends securely (picture A).

Twist: Divide dough into 2, shape into long rolls, twist together and secure the ends (picture B).

Cottage Loaf: Cut two-thirds off a piece of dough and make into a bun shape. Treat remaining part the same way; damp smaller one, place on top of the larger and secure by pushing your little finger right through the centre (picture C).

Knots: Shape into a long roll and knot (picture D).

5 Put rolls on the baking tray, cover and put in a warm place for 10–15 minutes, until doubled in size.

6 Brush the rolls with milk and bake until a rich golden-brown—about 15 minutes.

If you want to serve hot rolls you can make and shape the dough several hours beforehand (or overnight); just cover it and keep in the refrigerator, but remember to leave it at room temperature for 30–45 minutes to allow it to become soft before baking it as on opposite page.

APPLE CAKE

Ingredients
225 g self-raising flour
½ level tsp. cinnamon
100 g margarine
100 g soft brown sugar
2 eggs, beaten
50 g raisins, stoned or
  seedless
2 cooking apples,
  stewed and pulped

Utensils
Loaf tin 9 by 5 inches
  (23 by 12.5 cm)
Greaseproof paper
Cook's knife, tablespoon,
  teaspoon, wooden spoon
Sieve, mixing bowl
Plate
Small basin
Wire cooling rack

1 Heat the oven to 170°C. (325°F.), mark 3. Grease and line the loaf tin.

2 Sift together the flour and cinnamon.

3 Cream together the fat and sugar until light and fluffy.

4 Gradually add the beaten eggs.

5 Fold in half the sifted flour. Add the raisins and apple pulp and the remaining flour and fold in.

6 Turn the mixture into the prepared tin and bake just below the centre of the oven for about 1½ hours. Turn out, cool on wire rack and serve cut in slices and buttered.

SUPPER

Whether you serve supper or not depends on whether your main meal for the day is eaten at midday or in the evening. If you have your main meal at midday then high tea or a light supper should be sufficient.

If you are accustomed to eating your main meal in the evening a hot drink and biscuit at bedtime will be enough. If supper is to be one of your main meals the same points should be considered as for lunch:

1 Soup or a light starter may be served before the main course.

2 The meal should contain a protein dish, for example meat, fish, eggs, cheese.

3 Potatoes and two vegetables should be served if possible. Green vegetables or root vegetables are both nutritious and colourful. Alternatively serve a crisp green salad.

4 A second course is not absolutely necessary but can take the form of a light sweet, fresh or stewed fruit or alternatively cheese and biscuits.

CANNED AND PACKETED SOUPS

These days there are so many quick soups available that most people have some in their store-cupboards. Besides being made into soup, they can be used in other ways—for example, concentrated canned soup is fine undiluted as a sauce; just heat and serve. Good mixtures are: Tomato soup with sausages; Mushroom soup with fish; Celery soup with baked chicken.

Diluted soup may replace stock in stews or casseroles. To vary the standard flavours you can combine canned or packeted soup of two different flavours—for instance, Minestrone with cream of tomato; Green pea with mushroom; Chicken with rice plus celery, tomato or mushroom; Onion with pea or celery; Ox-tail with onion or tomato; Kidney with mushroom.

CHICKEN AND RICE SOUP

Ingredients	Utensils
1 onion	Vegetable knife
4 carrots	Cook's knife
1 stick of celery (if available)	Large saucepan
	Measuring jug
Carcase and scraps of a chicken left when main joints and breast have been removed	Sieve
	Bowl
	Plate
	Tablespoon
2 sprigs of parsley	
A bay leaf	
A few peppercorns	
Salt	
1 litre water	
50 g rice	
Chopped parsley	

1 Peel the onion and scrape the carrots, then cut each into 4 pieces. Cut up the celery, if used.

2 Put the chicken carcase in the saucepan, add the vegetables, parsley, bay leaf, peppercorns and salt and pour on the water.

3 Bring to the boil, put on the lid and simmer gently for 2–3 hours, or until the flesh has come away from the bones.

4 Put the sieve over the bowl and pour the stock through it. Leave the stock in the bowl to get cold.

5 Pick the pieces of chicken out of the sieve and put on to the plate. Throw away the remaining bones and vegetables.

6 When the stock is quite cold, skim all the fat from the surface, using a tablespoon.

7 Pour the stock back into the pan, bring to the boil, add the rice and boil for 25 minutes. Add the chicken pieces and boil for a further 5 minutes.

8 Serve sprinkled with chopped parsley.

If any giblet stock is left, add it to the chicken stock, straining it through the sieve into the bowl.

TOMATO SOUP

Ingredients	Utensils
25 g butter	Chopping board
1 stick of celery, washed and chopped	Vegetable knife
	Cook's knife
1 small onion, skinned and finely chopped	Large saucepan
	Measuring jug
1 carrot, pared and sliced	Sieve
1 rasher of bacon, chopped	Bowl
2 level tbsps. flour	Tablespoon
A bouquet garni	
700 g tomatoes, quartered	
500 ml stock	
Salt and pepper	
A little sugar	
Lemon juice	

1 Melt the butter and cook the celery, onion, carrot and bacon for 5 minutes.

2 Sprinkle in the flour and stir well.

3 Add the bouquet garni, tomatoes, stock and seasoning. Cover and cook gently for 30 minutes.

4 Sieve the soup, return it to the pan, check the seasoning, add a little sugar and lemon juice and reheat.

GRILLED HERRINGS

Ingredients	Utensils
4 fresh herrings	Newspaper
Salt and pepper	Cook's knife, scissors
	Grillpan and rack
	Spoon and fork

1 Heat the grill to a moderate heat.

2 Put the fish on a sheet of paper. If necessary, cut off the heads with a sharp knife (picture A) and remove the insides.

3 Rub salt inside the fish to remove any black skin, which tastes bitter if left (picture B).

4 Remove the scales by scraping with the knife from tail to head (picture C).

5 Using scissors, cut off fins and tail (picture D).

6 Wash the fish thoroughly in cold water and wipe dry.

7 Make 2 or 3 slanting cuts in the skin on each side of the fish (this is called " scoring ").

8 Sprinkle the herrings with salt and pepper.

9 Put the fish under the grill and cook for 10 minutes.

10 Using the spoon and fork, turn them over carefully and cook for a further 10 minutes. Serve at once.

STUFFED HERRINGS

Prepare 4 herrings as above. Mix 3 tbsps. fresh white breadcrumbs, 2 tsps. chopped parsley, $\frac{1}{2}$ a chopped onion, 2 peeled and chopped tomatoes, salt, pepper and 1 tbsp. milk in a basin. Stuff herrings, put in a greased dish, cover and bake in a 180°C. (350°F.), mark 4 oven for $\frac{1}{2}$ hour.

To bone a Herring

1 Using a sharp, pointed knife, split open each herring neatly down the underside.

2 Open out and place inner side downwards on a board.

3 Press lightly down middle of back with your fingers to loosen bones, but take care not to bruise the flesh.

4 Turn the fish over, ease the backbone up with your fingers and gently remove, with as many small bones as possible.

5 Cook any roes with the fish or use separately.

SCRAMBLED EGGS

Ingredients	Utensils
2 pieces of white bread	Plate
25 g butter	Round-bladed knife, fork,
2 eggs	tablespoon, wooden spoon
2 tbsps. milk	Saucepan
Salt and pepper	Basin

1 Heat the grill, then turn it low.

2 Toast the bread on both sides. Spread half the butter on the toast, put on a plate and keep warm under the grill.

3 Gently melt rest of butter in a saucepan (picture A).

4 Break the eggs into a basin, whisk with a fork, add the milk (picture B), season and mix thoroughly.

5 Pour into the saucepan and cook gently, stirring with the wooden spoon (picture C) till mixture begines to thicken.

6 Remove from the heat, but continue stirring until thick and creamy (picture D). Don't overheat, or the egg will become hard and break up.

7 Pile on the buttered toast and serve at once.

For a change, try one of these suggestions:

1 Chop 50 g bacon or 2 tomatoes and fry lightly in the butter before adding the eggs.

2 Stir one of the following into the cooked egg mixture:

$\frac{1}{2}$ level tsp. dried herbs or 1 level tsp. chopped fresh herbs; 75 g grated cheese; 50 g chopped ham.

BOILED EGGS

Simmer rather than boil the eggs, or the shells may break. Put into boiling water, lower heat and cook for 3–4$\frac{1}{2}$ minutes.

POACHED EGGS

If using a poacher, half-fill lower container with water and put a little butter in each cup. When water boils, break eggs into cups, sprinkle with salt and pepper and cover with lid.

Cook gently about 3 minutes; serve on buttered toast.
To use a frying pan, half-fill with water and add a pinch of
salt. Bring water to boil and put in 4 greased plain pastry
cutters. Break an egg into each cutter and cook gently till
set. Carefully remove cutters and lift out eggs with a slotted
spoon or slice; drain well.

A

B

C

D

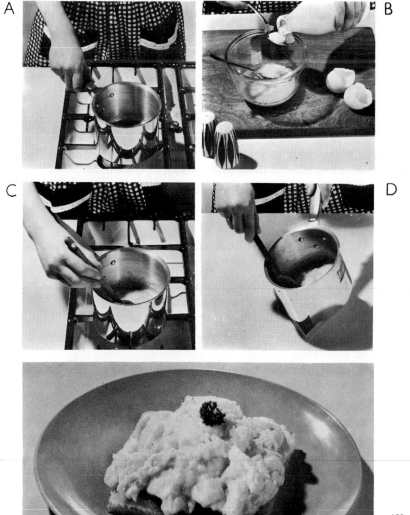

HAM AND EGG CHARLOTTE

Ingredients	Utensils
3 eggs	Small saucepan
2 thick slices of bread	Tablespoon, cook's knife,
50 g lean boiled ham	wooden spoon
50 g mushrooms	Basin
2 sticks of celery	Grater, plate
40 g margarine	Chopping board
40 g plain flour	Ovenproof dish
375 ml milk	Egg slicer, if available
Salt and pepper	Saucepan
Parsley	Measuring jug

1 Heat the oven to 180°C. (350°F.), mark 4.

2 Put the eggs in the pan and cover with cold water. Bring to the boil and boil for 10 minutes.

3 When the eggs are cooked, remove them from the boiling water and plunge them into a basin of cold water.

4 Remove crusts from bread and rub soft part on rough side of a grater placed over a plate to make crumbs (picture A).

5 Chop the ham and place it in the ovenproof dish.

6 Remove the shells from the eggs, slice them (picture B) and add to the ham, retaining 2–3 slices for garnish.

7 Chop the mushrooms and celery (picture C).

8 Melt 25 g of the fat in the saucepan, add the mushrooms and celery and cook for 10 minutes, or until soft.

9 Add the flour and mix with a wooden spoon, then remove the pan from the heat and add the milk gradually, stirring all the time; return the pan to the heat, bring to the boil and add salt and pepper to taste.

10 Pour this sauce over the eggs and ham (picture D), cover with breadcrumbs and dot with small pieces of butter.

11 Put towards the top of the oven and cook for 20–30 minutes, until the breadcrumbs are crisp and golden.

12 Garnish with the egg slices and parsley.

If you are in a hurry, do not make the sauce or add mushrooms and celery, but just pour a can of undiluted mushroom soup over the eggs and ham. Finish as opposite.
Ham and egg charlotte can be made several hours before you need it; put it into a cool place and reheat in a 180°C. (350°F.), mark 4 oven for 30 minutes.

A

B

C

D

CRISPY STUFFED ROLLS

Ingredients	Utensils
1 small onion	Grater, plate, chopping
50 g mushrooms	board
3 tomatoes	Cook's knife, tablespoon,
4 crisp dinner rolls	teaspoon, fork, wooden
25 g butter or margarine	spoon, vegetable knife
3 eggs	Small saucepan, frying pan
Salt and pepper	2 basins
	Baking sheet

1 Heat the oven to 180°C. (350°F.), mark 4.

2 Grate the onion on to a plate; chop the mushrooms.

3 Bring a pan of water to the boil, place the tomatoes in it and count up to 5; remove them to a bowl of cold water and peel off the skins (picture A). Chop the tomatoes.

4 Cut a round from top of rolls, using a sharp-pointed knife, then hollow out to leave crusty shells (picture B).

5 Melt butter in pan, add onion, mushrooms and tomatoes and sauté gently for 5–10 minutes, or until soft.

6 Beat the eggs with some salt and pepper in a basin with a fork, pour into the frying pan and stir with a wooden spoon over a low heat until the mixture thickens (picture C).

7 Pile the mixture into the bread shells, using a teaspoon (picture D), then replace the rounds of bread to form lids.

8 Put on a baking sheet and heat in the oven for 15 minutes, until the rolls are crisp and the filling hot.

SOFT STUFFED ROLLS

Ingredients	Utensils
1 small onion; 4 tomatoes	Grater
4 soft rolls	Plate
4 eggs	Chopping board
Salt and pepper	Cook's knife, vegetable knife
100 g cheese	Baking sheet

1 Heat the oven to 180°C. (350°F.), mark 4.

2 Grate the onion on to a plate; slice the tomatoes.
3 Cut a round from top of each roll and hollow out crust.
4 Put a little onion in each roll and add 2–3 tomato slices.
5 Break in an egg, then sprinkle with salt and pepper.
6 Grate cheese on a plate; sprinkle some on each roll.
7 Put rolls on baking sheet and bake for 20 minutes.

HAM AND LEEKS AU GRATIN

Ingredients

8 medium-sized leeks
Salt and pepper
100 g Cheddar cheese
A thick slice of bread
75 g margarine
50 g plain flour
250 ml milk
Nutmeg
8 slices of cooked ham
Parsley to garnish

Utensils

Vegetable knife, cook's
  knife, wooden spoon
Chopping board
Large and small saucepan
Colander, large basin
Measuring jug
Grater, 2 plates
Fireproof dish

1 Trim, wash and clean the leeks (picture A), put into boiling salted water and boil slowly for 20 minutes.

2 Drain the leeks in a colander over a large basin, pour 250 ml of the liquid into a measuring jug and leave to cool (picture B).

3 Grate the cheese on to a plate.

4 Holding the grater over a plate, rub the bread against it to make breadcrumbs.

5 Melt 50 g of the margarine in the small saucepan and remove from the heat. Add the flour, stir well with a wooden spoon, return the saucepan to the heat and cook gently until the mixture bubbles, then remove from the heat.

6 Add the milk and the leek liquid a little at a time, stirring thoroughly before adding any more.

7 Return the pan to the heat and bring to the boil, stirring all the time, until the sauce thickens.

8 Remove from the heat, add 50 g of the grated cheese and grate a little nutmeg into the mixture, then stir well.

9 Heat the grill.

10 Wrap each leek in a slice of ham and put in the fireproof dish (picture C).

11 Pour the sauce over the top and sprinkle with the remaining cheese and the breadcrumbs and some small pieces of margarine (picture D).

12 Put under the grill until golden-brown.

13 Chop the parsley and use to garnish the cooked dish.

A

B

C

D

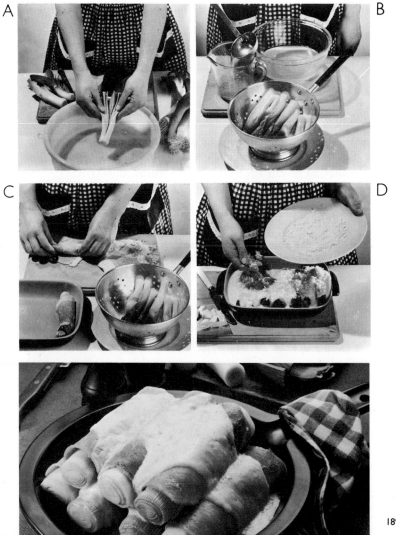

SAUSAGE ROLLS

Ingredients	Utensils
200 g plain flour	Sieve, mixing bowl
$\frac{1}{2}$ level tsp. salt	Teaspoon, round-bladed
100 g lard (*or* 50 g lard	knife
and 50 g margarine)	Plate, basin
Water to mix	Pastry board, dredger,
200 g sausage-meat	rolling pin, pastry brush
A little milk to glaze	Baking tray

1 Heat the oven to 200°C. (400°F.), mark 6.

2 Sift the flour and salt into a mixing bowl. Cut the fat into small pieces and rub into the flour until the mixture looks like fine breadcrumbs.

3 Add water 2 tsps. at a time, stirring with a round-bladed knife till mixture sticks together. Using one hand, collect together to give a firm dough and knead lightly.

4 Turn it on to a lightly floured board and shape into an oblong with the hands. Roll the pastry out thinly into an oblong (picture A), then cut lengthwise into 2 strips.

5 Divide the sausage-meat into 2 pieces and dust with flour. Using your hands, form into 2 rolls the length of the pastry strips (picture B).

6 Lay a roll of sausage-meat down centre of each strip, brush down edges of pastry with a little milk, fold one side of the pastry over the sausage-meat and press the two pastry edges firmly together (picture C).

7 Seal the long edges together by making small horizontal cuts with a round-bladed knife. Brush the length of the 2 rolls with milk, then cut each into slices 5 cm long (picture D).

8 Place on the baking tray and cook towards the top of the oven for 15 minutes; to cook the meat thoroughly without making the pastry too brown, lower the heat to 180°C. (350°F.), mark 4, and cook for a further 15 minutes.

Very good sausage rolls can be made with bought puff
pastry. Buy a 100 g packet and if possible keep it in the room
for 2 hours before using, then it will be easier to roll out.
Make the rolls as above, but heat oven to 220°C. (425°F.),
mark 7. Bake for 15 minutes, lower oven to 180°C. (350°F.),
mark 4, and bake for a further 15 minutes.

A

B

C

D

HAMBURGERS ON SAVOURY RICE

Ingredients

150 g rice
Salt and pepper
Parsley
50 g cooked ham
$\frac{1}{2}$ a red and $\frac{1}{2}$ a green
  pepper (optional)
50 g sultanas
Stock
8 hamburgers (frozen)
Oil

Utensils

Sieve
Large saucepan
Teaspoon, tablespoon,
  cook's knife
Chopping board
Flat ovenproof dish
Jug or measuring jug
Pastry brush
Greaseproof paper

1 Heat the oven to 180°C. (350°F.), mark 4.

2 Put the rice in a sieve and wash it under the cold tap.

3 Half-fill pan with water, bring to boil and add 2 level tsps. salt and rice. Boil rapidly for 5 minutes.

4 Chop the parsley finely; roughly chop the ham and the peppers (if used).

5 When the rice has been boiling for 5 minutes, drain it thoroughly in the sieve; put into the ovenproof dish.

6 Add the parsley, ham, peppers (if used), sultanas and some salt and pepper to the rice and mix well.

7 Add just enough stock to cover the rice (picture A).

8 Place the hamburgers on top of the rice and brush them over with oil (picture B); cover with a piece of greaseproof paper.

9 Cook in the centre of the oven for 45 minutes, or until all the liquid has been absorbed by the rice.

Try making your own **BACON-BURGERS**

Ingredients

200 g lean bacon
1 medium-sized onion
$\frac{1}{4}$ level tsp. dry mustard
$\frac{1}{4}$ level tsp. grated nutmeg

Pepper
Beaten egg
50 g lard

Utensils

Chopping board	Bowl
Cook's knife, fork, table- spoon	Frying pan

1 Mince bacon and onion or chop finely.

2 Mix bacon, onion, mustard, nutmeg and a shake of pepper. Add enough egg to make the mixture bind together.

3 Turn on to a floured board and shape into 8 cakes.

4 Fry in the hot lard in a frying pan for 6–7 minutes, turning the cakes 2 or 3 times with a fork and spoon.

A   B

CORNED BEEF CASSEROLE

Ingredients	Utensils
1 kg potatoes	Potato peeler or vegetable
Salt and pepper	knife, palette knife, table-
A medium-sized can	spoon, can opener
of corned beef	Large saucepan, frying pan
1 medium-sized onion	Chopping board
50 g margarine	Plate
A large can baked beans	Casserole

1 Heat the oven to 190°C. (375°F.), mark 5.

2 Peel the potatoes and cook in boiling salted water for about 20 minutes; drain and cut into dice (picture A).

3 Open the can of corned beef and cut into chunks.

4 Chop the onion.

5 Melt the margarine in the frying pan and add the diced potatoes; cook until lightly browned, then remove about a quarter of them on to a plate and put on one side to be used for topping (picture B).

6 Add onion to remaining potatoes and brown lightly.

7 Open the can of beans and stir into the mixture in the frying pan (picture C); add a good pinch of salt and pepper, then the chunks of meat, and mix well.

8 Transfer the mixture to the casserole and sprinkle the remaining diced potato over the top (picture D).

9 Bake in the oven for 20 minutes.

CURRY BEEF-BURGERS

Ingredients and Utensils	40 g margarine
500 g potatoes	1½ level tsps. curry
Salt and pepper	powder
A medium-sized can	50 g lard or dripping
of corned beef	Utensils as above,
1 medium-sized onion	excluding casserole

1 Cook the peeled potatoes in boiling salted water for 20 minutes, drain and mash them.

2 Cut the corned beef into chunks. Chop the onion.

3 Melt the margarine in the frying pan, add the onion and curry powder and fry until golden.

4 Stir in the meat and the onion mixture, then season.

5 When mixture is cool, shape in 8 cakes. Melt lard in frying pan and fry burgers on both sides until browned.

A

B

C

D

ICE CREAM

Ingredients	Utensils
150 ml milk	Ice tray
40 g caster sugar	Saucepan
2 eggs	Whisk
2.5–5 ml vanilla essence	Wooden spoon, metal spoon
150 ml double cream	Bowl
	Strainer

1 If you haven't a freezer set the refrigerator at lowest setting.

2 Heat the milk and sugar together in a saucepan, but do not boil.

3 Lightly beat the eggs and pour on the milk, stirring well.

4 Return the mixture to the saucepan and cook over a low heat, stirring all the time, until the mixture thickens to the consistency of custard.

5 Strain the custard into a bowl. Add the vanilla essence and allow to cool.

6 Whip the cream until half whipped. When the custard is cool gently fold the cream into the custard.

7 Pour into the ice tray and place in refrigerator or freezer.

8 When ice cream has frozen (1–2 hours depending on refrigerator or freezer) turn it into a mixing bowl and whisk thoroughly. Return it to the ice tray and replace in refrigerator or freezer until completely frozen.

Variations
Chocolate: Add 40 g melted chocolate when folding in cream.
Coffee: Add 10 ml powdered coffee dissolved in 5 ml hot water.
Banana: Add 2 small bananas, mashed or puréed.

ICE CREAM AND A HOT SAUCE

Chocolate Sauce: Break up 50 g plain chocolate into small pieces, add 15 g butter and place in a basin over a saucepan of water. Heat the water gently until the chocolate and butter melt, then stir in 1 tbsp. milk and 1 tsp. vanilla essence. Pour the hot sauce over cubes of ice cream.

Butterscotch Sauce: Put 25 g butter, 1 level tbsp. Demerara sugar and 1 tbsp. golden syrup in a saucepan and heat gently until they melt. Boil for 1 minute, then, if liked, stir in 25 g chopped walnuts. Pour while still hot over cubes of ice cream.

BELLE HELENE PEARS

425 g can pear halves
Vanilla ice cream (see basic recipe)
Chocolate sauce (see above)
Whipped cream

Drain the juice from the can of pears. Put portions of ice cream in 4 individual glasses. Add a pear half to each and spoon some of the sauce over. Decorate the top with whipped cream.

COFFEE, TEA, MILKY DRINKS

TEA

Ingredients

Utensils

Boiling water
Sugar
Milk
Tea

Kettle, tea-pot, hot-water
jug
Milk jug, sugar basin
Cups, saucers, teaspoons

1 Fill the kettle from the cold-water tap and put it on to boil.

2 Pour the milk into the jug and put some sugar in the bowl.

3 When the water in the kettle is hot pour a little of it into the tea-pot and hot-water jug (which are placed on the table) and leave them to warm. Return the kettle to the heat.

4 Throw away the water from the pot and jug and put the tea in the pot, allowing about 1 tsp. per person.

5 Pour on really boiling water, three-quarters filling the pot.

6 Fill the hot-water jug with boiling water.

7 Leave the tea for 2 minutes before pouring it out. Add milk and sugar to the cups as desired. Refill the tea-pot with hot water.

COFFEE

Ingredients

Utensils

Boiling water
50 g ground coffee (2
  rounded tbsps.)
375 ml milk
Demerara sugar

Kettle, coffee pot, milk jug
Tablespoon
Measuring jug
Milk pan, strainer

1 Put a kettle of water on to boil. Put the milk jug to warm.

2 Pour some of the hot water into the coffee pot and return the kettle to the heat; empty and dry the pot. Put the coffee into the measuring jug.

3 Pour 500 ml boiling water on to the coffee, stir very thoroughly and leave to stand for about 5 minutes.

4 Meanwhile heat the milk in the pan until almost on the point of boiling, then pour it into the warmed jug. Keep it hot.

5 Strain the coffee into the hot pot (or into a pan if it has to be reheated).

6 Serve the coffee and milk in the separate jugs, so that they can be mixed to suit each person. Add sugar to the cups as required.

MILKY DRINKS

Follow the instructions on the tin, but do remember:

1 Don't have the milk boiling or a skin will form.

2 Don't have a lid on the milk pan, or you won't be able to watch it carefully and it may boil over.

3 Always soak the pan in cold water immediately after use, to make cleaning easier.

CHELSEA BUNS

Ingredients
1 level tsp. sugar
150 ml milk
2 level tsps. dried yeast
200 g plain flour
½ level tsp. salt
25 g lard or margarine
25 g softened butter
25 g dried fruit
25 g sugar
1 tbsp. milk for glaze

Utensils
Teaspoon, wooden spoon,
  round-bladed knife
Measuring jug
Sieve, mixing bowl
An 8-in (20 cm) round
  cake tin
Pastry board, dredger,
  rolling pin
Small basin
Small saucepan

1 Stir 1 tsp. sugar into the milk; sprinkle on the yeast and leave for 10–15 minutes, until frothy.

2 Meanwhile, sift the flour and salt into the mixing bowl and rub in the fat.

3 Make a hole in the flour, pour in the milk and yeast, then, using a wooden spoon, gradually mix in the flour and beat well until smooth. Cover with a cloth and put in a warm place to rise until twice the original size.

4 Grease the cake tin.

5 Turn the risen dough out on to a floured board and knead it lightly.

6 Roll out into a 25 cm square. Spread the butter evenly over the dough, using the round-bladed knife. Sprinkle with the fruit and sugar.

7 Damp the edges and roll up firmly, like a Swiss roll (picture A).

8 Press together tightly and cut the roll into 8 slices; put into the greased tin, cut side uppermost (picture B).

9 Allow to prove in a warm place for 15–20 minutes until twice the size. Heat the oven to 220°C. (425°F.), mark 7.

10 Bake the buns for 10 minutes, reduce the heat to 190°C. (375°F.), mark 5 and cook for a further 10 minutes, until golden-brown.

11 Meanwhile boil 1 tbsp. water and 2 tsps. sugar in a pan until syrupy. Brush the buns as soon as they come from the oven, so that the syrup dries on.

Alternatively, omit the glaze and when the buns are baked and cold, brush the tops over with glacé icing (see page 142) made with 100 g icing sugar.

12 Break the buns apart when cool.

A

B

BANBURY CAKES

Ingredients	Utensils
1 large pkt. frozen puff pastry	Sieve
50 g currants	Plate
50 g stoned raisins	Tablespoon, teaspoon
1 level tbsp. flour	Basin
25 g chopped candied peel	Small saucepan (*or* lemon squeezer)
50 g Demerara sugar	Pastry board, dredger, rolling pin, pastry brush
½ level tsp. cinnamon	A 5-in (13 cm) plain cutter (*or* saucepan lid)
½ level tsp. nutmeg	Baking tray
25 g butter (*or* ½ a lemon —1 tbsp. juice)	
A little milk or egg white	
1–2 tbsps. caster sugar	

1 Heat the oven to 220°C. (425°F.), mark 7. Leave the pastry at room temperature until it is soft.

2 Place the currants and raisins in a sieve with the flour and shake well over a plate so that any bits or stalks from the fruit pass through to the plate. Mix the fruit with the candied peel, sugar and spices in a basin.

3 Melt the butter, or squeeze the juice from the lemon and measure off 1 tbsp. Stir into the fruit mixture and mix well.

4 Roll out the pastry thinly on a floured board and cut into rounds with the cutter or lid (picture A).

5 Place 1 level tbsp. of the fruit mixture in the centre of each pastry round. Brush the edges of the pastry with milk or egg white, draw them up to the centre and press well to enclose the filling (picture B).

6 Turn the cakes over and roll out lightly until the fruit just shows under the pastry and the cakes are oval in shape (picture C). Make several cuts in the top of each cake, forming a criss-cross pattern.

7 Brush with milk or egg white and sprinkle with a little sugar. Put on baking tray (picture D) and bake towards top of oven for about 20 minutes, or until the pastry is golden.

ECCLES CAKES

These are very similar to Banbury Cakes, but the fruit used in the filling is only currants, not a mixture, and the cakes are round. The tops of the cakes are decorated with 3 small cuts.

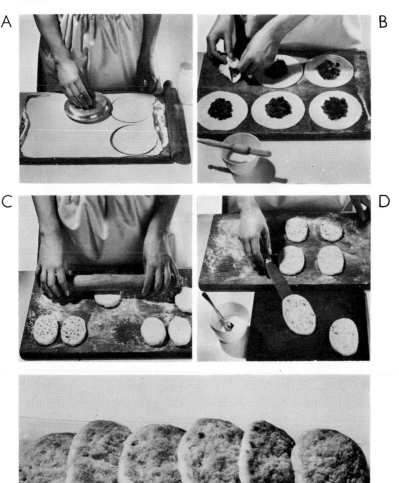

A

B

C

D

MADEIRA CAKE

Ingredients

200 g plain flour
1 level tsp. baking powder
1 lemon
150 g butter
150 g caster sugar
3 eggs
Citron peel (optional)

Utensils

6-in (15 cm) round cake tin
Greaseproof paper, pencil, scissors
Sieve, 2 plates
Teaspoon, tablespoon, wooden spoon, fork, round-bladed knife
Grater
Mixing bowl, basin

1 Heat the oven to 180°C. (350°F.), mark 4. Grease the cake tin, line with greaseproof paper, then grease the paper.

2 Sift the flour and baking powder on to a plate. Grate the rind from the lemon, standing the grater on a plate and using the rough side.

3 Using a wooden spoon, cream the fat and sugar with the lemon rind in a mixing bowl, until the mixture is pale, soft and fluffy.

4 Crack the eggs into a basin and whisk with a fork. Add the egg 2 tsps. at a time to the creamed fat and sugar, beating until well mixed in before adding any more.

5 Fold in half the flour, using a tablespoon, until well mixed in, then fold in the remaining flour.

6 Turn the mixture into the prepared cake tin (picture A) and level the top. Place near the bottom of the oven, cover the top of the cake with a piece of greaseproof paper and bake for about $1\frac{1}{2}$ hours, or until well risen, firm and golden.

7 Traditionally, this cake is decorated with 2 strips of candied citron peel, which are stuck into the top of the cake after it has been cooking for about $\frac{1}{2}$ hour (picture B).

Notes: As this cake does not contain any fruit, many people refer to it as a " plain " cake, but this is wrong—it is " rich ", because it has a high proportion of fat and sugar to the amount of flour.

The recipe can be varied in various ways, although it will no longer give a traditional Madeira cake. Here are two suggestions:

1 *Orange Cake:* Add the grated rind of 2 oranges.

2 *Rich Cherry Cake:* Add 100 g glacé cherries; cut each cherry in half, wash in warm water to remove any syrup (which would make them sink in the cake), then dry really well before adding.

3 *Almond, Walnut or Hazel Cake:* Add 50 g nuts, blanched and chopped.

A   B

BAKEWELL TART

Ingredients

1 small pkt. frozen puff
  pastry
3 small sponge cakes
75 g ground almonds
$\frac{1}{2}$ a lemon
50 g butter or margarine
50 g caster sugar
1 egg
1–2 tbsps. raspberry jam

Utensils

Sieve, basin, mixing bowl
Grater, plate
Lemon squeezer
Pastry board, dredger,
  rolling pin
Round-bladed knife, table-
  spoon, teaspoon, fork,
  wooden spoon
A 7-in (18 cm) pie plate
Baking tray

1 Heat the oven to 220°C. (425°F.), mark 7. Leave the pastry at room temperature until it is soft.

2 Crumble the sponge cakes into a sieve over a basin, then rub them through to give fine crumbs (picture A). Sift the ground almonds also and mix with the crumbs.

3 Stand the grater on a plate and grate the rind from the lemon, using the rough side of the grater. Squeeze out the lemon juice.

4 Form the pastry into a round with the hands and roll out on a lightly floured board into a round 1 cm larger all round than the pie plate. Line the plate with the pastry, taking care not to stretch it; trim off pastry edges.

5 Put the fat, sugar and grated lemon rind into the bowl and cream with a wooden spoon until mixture is soft, pale and fluffy.

6 Break the egg into a basin and whisk lightly with fork. Add the egg 2 tsps. at a time to the creamed fat and sugar, beating until well mixed in before adding any more (picture B).

7 Lightly fold in cake crumbs and almonds with a table-spoon (picture C), adding a little lemon juice if necessary to make the mixture soft enough to drop easily from the spoon when this is held above the bowl and shaken.

8 Spread the base of the pastry with jam and cover evenly with the creamed mixture (picture D).

9 Put tart on a baking tray and bake towards top of oven for about 15 minutes, or until pastry sets, then reduce to 180°C. (350°F.), mark 4 and cook for a further 30 minutes, until filling is well risen, firm and golden.

A

B

C

D

SHORTBREAD

Ingredients

150 g plain flour
50 g caster sugar
100 g butter
Caster sugar for dredging
  shortbread

Utensils

Baking tray
Sieve, mixing bowl
Pastry board, dredger,
  rolling pin
Round-bladed knife, fork
Cooling rack

1 Heat the oven to 150°C. (300°F.), mark 1–2. Grease the baking tray.

2 Sift the flour and sugar together into a mixing bowl.

3 Work the butter into the dry ingredients by squeezing gently with one hand, keeping the fat in one piece until the mixture binds together.

4 Turn the dough on to a lightly floured board, divide evenly into 2 and press each piece into a round shape; roll each lightly to 1 cm thick, still keeping the round shape.

5 Crimp the edges with the finger and thumb, mark each round into 6–8 sections with knife and prick the surface with a fork.

6 Place the rounds on the greased baking tray and bake in the centre of the oven for about 45 minutes, until firm and lightly browned.

7 When the shortbreads are cooked, lift them carefully on to the cooling rack and dredge with caster sugar.

8 When they are cool, divide into pieces.

The recipes in this chapter are a few of the many recipes in this country that are traditionally made at certain times of the year.

EASTER BISCUITS

Ingredients	Utensils
75 g margarine	2 baking trays
50 g caster sugar	Bowl
1 egg, separated	Sieve, plate
175 g self-raising flour	Wooden spoon, tablespoon
A pinch of salt	Pastry board, flour dredger,
35 g currants	rolling pin, pastry brush
15 g mixed peel, chopped	A 2-in (5-cm) round cutter
1–2 tbsps. milk	Wire cooling rack
A little caster sugar	

1 Heat the oven to 150°C. (300°F.), mark 1–2. Grease the baking tray.

2 Cream the margarine and sugar and beat in the egg yolk.

3 Sift the flour with the salt and fold into the creamed mixture, with the currants and mixed peel. Add enough milk to give a fairly soft dough, cover and leave in a cool place to become firm.

4 Knead lightly on a floured board and roll out 0.5 cm thick.

5 Cut into rounds with the cutter, and put on the baking trays and bake in the centre of the oven: after 10 minutes baking brush the biscuits with the egg white, sprinkle with sugar and continue cooking for a further 10 minutes, until lightly coloured.

6 Remove from the oven and cool on a wire cooling rack.

SIMNEL CAKE

Ingredients

550 g bought almond
  paste
300 g currants
100 g sultanas
75 g mixed candied peel
200 g plain flour
A pinch of salt
1 level tsp. ground
  cinnamon
1 level tsp. ground nutmeg
150 g butter
150 g caster sugar
3 eggs
Milk to mix

Utensils

A 7-in (18 cm) round
  cake tin
Greaseproof paper
Pastry board, rolling pin,
  pastry brush
Sieve, plate
Cook's knife, tablespoon,
  teaspoon, fork, wooden
  spoon, round-bladed knife
Chopping board
2 mixing bowls
Basin

1 Grease the cake tin, line with greaseproof paper and grease the paper.

2 Divide the almond paste into 3; take one portion and roll it out to a round the size of the cake tin.

3 Place the currants and sultanas in a sieve, sprinkle over them 1 tbsp. of the flour and shake well over a plate, so that any stalks or bits from the fruit pass through on to the plate. Put the mixed peel and prepared fruit into a mixing bowl.

4 Sift together the flour, salt and spices and add to the fruit and peel.

5 Heat the oven to 150°C. (300°F.), mark 1–2.

6 Cream the butter and sugar, using a wooden spoon, until the mixture is pale, soft and fluffy.

7 Break the eggs into a basin and whisk lightly with a fork. Add the egg 2 tsps. at a time to the creamed fat and sugar, beating until well mixed each time before adding any more egg.

8 Using a tablespoon, fold in the flour and fruit mixture; add a little milk if required to make the mixture soft enough to drop easily from the spoon when this is held above the bowl and shaken.

9 Put half the mixture into the prepared tin, smooth and cover with the round of almond paste. Put the remaining cake mixture on top.

10 Bake in the centre of the oven for about $3\frac{1}{2}$ to 4 hours, until the cake is golden-brown and firm to the touch and no longer " sings ". Cool in the cake tin before removing.

11 Take another third of the almond paste and roll out to a round the size of the tin; make small balls from the remaining third—eleven is the traditional number.

12 Heat the grill.

13 Cover the top of the cake with the round of paste and place the small balls round the edge. Brush the paste with any remaining beaten egg and brown under the grill.

14 Alternatively, coat top of cake with glacé icing, made by mixing 3 tbsps. sieved icing sugar with a little cold water until it will coat the back of the spoon.

15 Decorate with a tiny chick or a few sugar eggs.

Can you find out the origin of this cake ?

HOT CROSS BUNS

Ingredients

Utensils

55 g sugar
125 ml warm milk
2 level tsps. dried yeast
300 g plain flour
½ level tsp. salt
25 g margarine or lard
½ level tsp. mixed spice
25 g dried fruit
1 egg, beaten
25 g fat and 50 g plain
  flour for pastry crosses
50 g sugar and 2 tbsps.
  milk for glaze

Teaspoon, tablespoon,
  wooden spoon, round-
  bladed knife, fork
Measuring jug
Sieve, mixing bowl
Small basin
Baking tray
Pastry board,
  dredger, rolling pin,
  pastry brush
Small saucepan

These are traditionally eaten at breakfast on Good Friday.

1 Stir 5 g sugar into the milk; sprinkle on the yeast and leave for 10–15 minutes, until frothy.

2 Meanwhile sift flour and salt into mixing bowl and rub in fat. Stir in the 50 g sugar, spice and fruit.

3 Break egg into a basin and whisk lightly with fork.

4 Make a hole in the flour and pour in the milk and yeast and the egg. Using a wooden spoon, gradually work in the flour to form a soft dough. Beat well until smooth, cover with a cloth and put to rise.

5 Grease the baking tray.

6 When the dough is risen, turn it out on to a floured board and knead lightly. Divide into 9 pieces. Flour your hands and form each piece to a round shape; flatten slightly and put on the baking tray.

7 Cover and leave in a warm place until twice the size. Heat the oven to 220°C. (425°F.), mark 7.

8 Rub the remaining 25 g fat into the 50 g plain flour and add a little cold water, until the mixture forms a firm dough.

Knead lightly, then roll out thinly on a floured board and cut into thin strips 5 cm long (picture A).

9 Dissolve the 50 g sugar in 2 tbsps. milk in the pan and boil until syrupy, to make a glaze.

10 When the buns have proved, damp the strips of pastry and lay 2 on each bun to make a cross (picture B).

11 Bake for 15–20 minutes, until golden-brown and firm to the touch. Brush at once with glaze and allow to cool.

Note: If time is short, omit the pastry crosses and mark a cross on each bun by making 2 deep cuts.

A

B

MINCEMEAT

Ingredients	Utensils
100 g stoned raisins	Cook's knife, teaspoon,
100 g currants	wooden spoon
100 g sultanas	Chopping board
50 g mixed candied peel	Large mixing bowl
100 g apples	Grater, plate
1 lemon	Lemon squeezer
50 g shelled walnuts	2 small jam jars
200 g Demerara sugar	1 pkt. jam covers and labels
100 g suet	Saucer
$\frac{1}{2}$ level tsp. mixed spice	
2 tbsps. brandy	

1 Chop the raisins and place with the other fruit and the peel in the mixing bowl.

2 Peel, quarter and core apples and chop finely, or grate on a grater standing in a basin; add to other fruit.

3 Grate rind from lemon on to a plate; cut fruit in half and remove juice, using the lemon squeezer.

4 Add the grated rind and the juice and all the other ingredients to the mixture; stir thoroughly.

5 Fill the jam jars right to the top (picture A). Cover mincemeat with waxed paper discs, pressing down firmly so that no air bubbles remain trapped beneath the paper.

6 Put some water in the saucer. Dip a cloth in the water and use to damp one side of a Cellophane jar cover. Carefully stretch the cover over the top of the jar (picture B) and secure with an elastic band. Make sure there are no creases or puckers across the top. Cover all the jars in the same way.

7 Label the jars clearly, adding the date.

Notes: Use clean, dry fruit, or the mincemeat will ferment quickly. However, never clean the fruit by rubbing it in flour—this makes the mixture ferment even sooner. Before using mincemeat, remember to stir well, as the top tends to dry out while the bottom part is very juicy.

If during storage mincemeat shows signs of becoming bubbly and develops a winy smell, it is said to be fermenting. To correct this, tip it all out of the jars into a large pan and bring slowly to the boil, stirring occasionally. Boil for 1 minute, then re-pot and cover in the usual way.

Mincemeat is used in many ways—in pies (see p. 216), mincemeat slices, as a stuffing for baked apples, in an open tart decorated with a lattice of pastry or as a layer in a steamed pudding. Another variation is to line a greased pudding basin with mincemeat, fill with a sponge pudding mixture and steam in the usual way.

A

B

MINCE PIES

Ingredients	Utensils
200 g plain flour	Sieve, mixing bowl
½ level tsp. salt	Basin
100 g lard (*or* 50 g lard	Teaspoon, round-bladed
and 50 g margarine)	knife
Water to mix	Pastry board, dredger,
Mincemeat	rolling pin, pastry brush
A little milk to glaze	2 round cutters
	Trays of patty tins
	Cooling rack

1 Heat the oven to 220°C. (425°F.), mark 7.

2 Sift the flour and salt into a mixing bowl and add the fat, cut in small pieces. Rub it in, using your fingertips, until the mixture is like fine breadcrumbs.

3 Add the water 2 tsps. at a time, stirring with the round-bladed knife until the mixture sticks together. Using one hand, collect it together to give a firm dough and knead lightly until smooth.

4 Turn it on to a lightly floured board, cut into 2 equal pieces and roll out one thinly. Using a cutter slightly bigger than the top of the patty tins, cut into rounds.

5 Place one round in each patty tin, pressing it well in but trying not to stretch the pastry.

6 Roll out remaining pastry and, using a cutter just a little smaller, cut out more rounds (picture A). The trimmings of pastry can then all be kneaded together and re-rolled to give more pastry rounds (though when cooked these will tend to be slightly less tender than those from the first rolling).

7 Put a good tsp. of mincemeat in each patty case. Brush the edges of the smaller rounds with water and put over the mincemeat, dampened side downwards, pressing the edges firmly together to seal them well (picture B).

8 Make 2 cuts in the top of each tart. Brush the tops with a little milk and bake toward the top of the oven for about 20 minutes, or until the pastry is firm and golden.

9 Remove from the tins at once and leave on the cooling rack. Before serving, reheat in a 180°C. (350°F.), mark 4 oven for about 10 minutes and sprinkle with sieved icing sugar.

Note: Frozen puff pastry (a 212 g pkt.) may be used instead of shortcrust pastry, but the mince pies should then be brushed if possible with a little beaten egg instead of milk, to give a really glazed finish.

A   B

CHRISTMAS CAKE

<table>
<tr><td>

Ingredients

450 g currants
200 g sultanas
200 g stoned raisins
150 g glacé cherries
100 g mixed candied peel
$\frac{1}{2}$–1 lemon
250 g plain flour
A pinch of salt
$\frac{1}{2}$ level tsp. mixed spice
$\frac{1}{2}$ level tsp. cinnamon
250 g butter
250 g soft brown sugar
6 eggs
3 tbsps. milk

</td><td>

Utensils

Sieve
Tea towel, kitchen paper,
  tray
9-in (22 cm) round cake tin
Greaseproof paper, brown
  paper, pencil, scissors,
  string
Cook's knife, wooden spoon,
  fork, teaspoon, tablespoon,
  round-bladed knife
Chopping board
3 mixing bowls
Grater
Basin

</td></tr>
</table>

Make the cake as long as possible beforehand, to let it " mature ", becoming darker in colour and richer in flavour; it is best made at the beginning of November, but if necessary can be made as late as a fortnight before Christmas.

1 2–3 days beforehand, wash the dried fruit in a sieve under the cold tap. Drain well, turn on to a clean tea towel, pat dry, spread out on kitchen paper and leave to dry.

2 On the day, grease the cake tin, line it with double greaseproof paper and re-grease. Tie a band of brown paper round the outside of the tin, to come 8 cm above the top.

3 Mix the prepared fruit, peel and cherries in the bowl.

4 Grate the lemon rind into the bowl of fruit.

5 Heat the oven to 150°C. (300°F.), mark 1–2.

6 Continue as for Simnel Cake, p. 210, stages 4, 6 (where lemon rind should be added), 7, 8.

7 Turn the mixture into the prepared tin, spread it evenly with a round-bladed knife and make a dip in the centre.

8 Bake towards bottom of oven for about $4\frac{1}{2}$ hours, until the cake is rich golden-brown and firm to the touch and no longer " sings "; when a fine skewer is inserted this should look quite clean as it is drawn out.

9 To prevent top of cake over-browning cover with several thicknesses of brown paper after the first 2½ hours.

10 Allow cake to cool in the tin.

11 To give a richer flavour prick the cake with a fine skewer and slowly pour 2–3 tbsps. brandy over before storing.

12 To store the cake wrap it in several layers of greaseproof paper, then put it in an airtight tin or wrap it in foil.

13 Put on almond paste and royal icing, then decorate as you like—see the following pages. If possible, leave for a week—or at the very least for 24 hours—after putting on the almond paste, or the oil from the almonds may stain the royal icing yellow.

DECORATING A CHRISTMAS CAKE
ALMOND PASTE

Ingredients	Utensils
325 g icing sugar	Sieve
325 g ground almonds	Mixing bowl
1 egg	Basin
1 tsp. vanilla essence	Fork, wooden spoon
1½ tbsps. lemon juice	Lemon squeezer

Note: If top of cake only is to be covered, as in picture on page 219, make half the above quantity of paste.

1 Sift sugar into bowl and add the almonds.

2 Break egg into basin and whisk lightly with fork.

3 Stir egg into sugar and almonds; add vanilla essence and enough lemon juice to give a stiff dough.

4 Form into a ball and knead lightly.

How to put Almond Paste on a Cake

1 Sieve 200 g apricot jam.

2 Trim top of cake if necessary; brush cake well with jam.

3 Measure round the cake, using a piece of string.

4 Divide the almond paste into 2 equal portions. Halve one piece again and form each quarter-portion into a roll; Roll out each roll half as long as the length of the measuring string and as wide as the cake is deep.

5 Press the strips firmly on to the sides of the cake (picture A), smoothing the joins with a round-bladed knife and keeping the edges square (picture B). Roll the cake edgewise on the table top to straighten the sides.

6 Brush the top rim of the paste with jam.

7 Dredge the board heavily with icing sugar, then roll out remaining almond paste to fit the top of the cake.

8 Turn the cake upside down, centre it exactly on the round of paste, press down firmly, then smooth the join.

9 Loosen paste from board and turn cake right way up. Check that top edge is quite level (picture C).

Easy Almond Paste Decorations: Choose a design with a simple, fairly bold outline—stars, candles, the Christmas trees seen on p. 217 or the holly leaves on p. 223. Draw the shape on stiff paper and cut out. Colour some almond paste by working edible colouring in evenly; roll out very thinly on a board sprinkled with icing sugar and cut round the pattern with a sharp-pointed knife. For holly berries, roll tiny balls of red-tinted paste. Leave the shapes on a plate till quite dry, then stick them on to firm royal icing with a dab of fresh icing. Cover the cake lightly to prevent dust settling on it.

A

B

DECORATING A CHRISTMAS CAKE (Continued)
ROYAL ICING

Ingredients
900 g icing sugar
4 egg whites
2 tsps. glycerine

Utensils
Sieve, 2 mixing bowls
Fork, wooden spoon, tea-
spoon
Damp cloth, greaseproof
paper

Note: If top only of cake is iced, use half above amounts.

1 Sift sugar into a mixing bowl.

2 Stir egg whites with a fork in another bowl just sufficiently to break them up, but don't include too much air.

3 Add 450 g sugar; using wooden spoon, mix well; stir briskly for 10 minutes, or until smooth, glossy and white.

4 Cover with damp cloth or greaseproof paper and leave for at least 1 hour, to let any bubbles rise to surface.

5 Gradually add rest of sugar till required consistency is reached; the mixture should be stiff enough for peaks to form easily on surface when you " pull " it up with spoon.

6 Add the glycerine.

7 If possible, leave the icing overnight in an airtight container in a cool place before using it.

8 For a really smooth result, just before using the icing, remove 1 tbsp. of it, mix to a coating consistency with water, return it to the rest and mix until smooth.

To Put on the Icing

1 Put 1 tsp. icing on an 11-in (28 cm) cake board and place the cake firmly in the centre of the board.

2 Spoon the icing on top of the cake; working with a palette knife in a to-and-fro motion until the air bubbles are broken, cover the top and sides of the cake evenly. If top only is iced, be sure to cover almond paste at sides.

3 Draw a clean ruler or palette knife across top of cake, evenly and steadily, till surface is quite smooth (picture A).

4 Using a plastic scraper, smooth sides (picture B).

To Rough-ice and Decorate the Cake

1 As shown below: Using a round-bladed knife, draw icing up into peaks around sides and in a 4 cm border round top of cake. When dry, add holly berries and leaves.

2 As seen on page 217: Rough-ice as above in a border round edge and top of sides. When firm, put ribbon round cake just below icing; cut it just long enough to overlap, pin in place with 2 dressmaking pins, then make a bow (by folding the ribbon rather than tying it) and pin this in place. Add the almond paste Christmas trees.

CHRISTMAS PUDDING

Ingredients	Utensils
100 g sultanas	900-ml basin
50 g currants	2 mixing bowls, 1 small bowl
100 g stoned raisins	Wooden spoon
150 g flour	Whisk
12.5 ml salt	Steamer
75 g fresh breadcrumbs	Greaseproof paper
75 g suet	Foil
5 ml mixed spice	
A little grated nutmeg	
75 g sugar	
2 eggs	
15 ml syrup	
15 ml marmalade	
A little milk or water	
A few drops of vanilla essence	
A few drops of almond essence	
A little browning	

1 Grease the 900-ml pudding basin.

2 Wash and dry the dried fruit.

3 Put flour, salt and breadcrumbs into a bowl.

4 Add suet, spices and sugar and mix well.

5 Add the dried fruits and mix well.

6 Lightly beat the eggs. Pour in together with syrup, marmalade and enough milk or water to give a soft dropping consistency.

7 Stir in the essences and enough browning to colour it.

8 Put into the basin, it should be nearly full. Cover with greased greaseproof paper and foil and steam for 6 hours.

9 Steam for a further 2 hours before serving.

There are many exciting recipes from all over the world that have become familiar to us during holidays abroad and by people from other countries coming to live here.

Unusual vegetables and spices are now imported and available in our shops. These enable us to experiment and try the unusual and different flavours of foods from other countries.

VICHYSSOISE SOUP

Ingredients	Utensils
1 onion, skinned	Chopping board
2 potatoes, thinly sliced	Large saucepan and lid
4 leeks	Sieve
50 g butter	Wooden spoon, cook's knife
Salt and pepper	
1½ litres stock	
300 ml cream	
Chopped chives to garnish	

1 Peel the onion and potatoes; wash the leeks. Slice the onion, potatoes and leeks finely with the cook's knife.

2 Melt the butter in the saucepan and lightly fry the leeks and onions for about 10 minutes, until soft but not coloured.

3 Add the seasoning, stock and potatoes, cover and cook until the vegetables are soft.

4 Sieve the soup, stir in the cream, with more seasoning if necessary, and chill.

5 Sprinkle with chives before serving.

SPAGHETTI BOLOGNESE

Ingredients	Utensils
1 small onion	Vegetable knife, cook's
1 small carrot	knife, wooden spoon,
2 sticks of celery	teaspoon
4 tomatoes	Chopping board
40 g butter	Saucepan and lid, large
225 g minced raw beef	saucepan
250 ml bouillon cube stock	Large shallow serving dish
Salt and pepper	Measuring jug
200 g spaghetti	Sieve

1 Peel the onion and carrot; scrub the celery; skin the tomatoes. Chop the onion, carrot and celery finely with a cook's knife; chop the tomatoes.

2 Melt 25 g of the butter in a saucepan, add the onion, carrot and celery and fry gently for 5 minutes, stirring so that the mixture does not stick or burn.

3 Stir in the meat and fry for another 5 minutes.

4 Add the stock to pan, with tomatoes, salt and pepper. Cover with a lid and leave to simmer for 30 minutes.

5 Meanwhile half-fill a large saucepan with water, bring to the boil and add 1 level tsp. salt. Put the serving dish to warm.

6 Dip one end of the spaghetti into the water, wait until it softens, then wind it round and round in the water until it is completely covered (picture A).

7 Boil quickly for 20 minutes, or until just tender. Pour into a sieve to drain off the water (picture B). Return it to the pan and stir in the remaining butter so that it coats the spaghetti.

8 Place the spaghetti on the hot serving dish and pour the meat sauce over.

Notes: Spaghetti is one of a group of foods, which also includes macaroni, that are known collectively as Pasta.

Italians eat pasta instead of potatoes.

In Italy 1 clove of garlic (finely chopped) is often fried with the vegetables and a pinch of nutmeg and a bay leaf may be added with the salt and pepper, to give a more highly seasoned sauce; 1–2 tbsps. tomato purée (paste) is often used instead of fresh tomatoes.

It is traditional in Italy to serve Spaghetti Bolognese with a small dish of grated Parmesan cheese. In this country, finely grated Cheddar cheese could be used instead, although it is possible to buy small tins of Parmesan cheese at many grocers.

RISOTTO

Ingredients	Utensils
1 onion	Cook's knife, vegetable
50 g flat mushrooms	knife, wooden spoon
50 g margarine	Chopping board
200 g long-grain (Patna)	Sieve
rice	Saucepan and lid
750 ml bouillon cube	Measuring jug
stock	Grater, plate
25 g Parmesan or	
Cheddar cheese	

1 Peel the onion; wash the mushrooms in a sieve and drain them well. Chop the onion finely and slice the mushrooms.

2 Melt the margarine in a saucepan, add onion and mushrooms (picture A) and fry for about 5 minutes, or until golden-brown. Meanwhile, place the rice in the sieve, rinse in cold water and drain.

3 Add the rice to the vegetable mixture in the saucepan (picture B) and heat gently, stirring until all the margarine has been taken up.

4 Pour the stock over the rice and stir well.

5 Cover pan with a tight-fitting lid and simmer gently for about 20 minutes, or till all the water has been absorbed.

6 Meanwhile, grate the cheese on to a plate, using the fine holes on the grater. When the risotto is ready, stir in the cheese. Serve at once.

Note: This is the basic risotto, which can be varied in many ways for example:

Rind 50 g streaky bacon and chop the rashers in 1 cm strips. Add these when you are frying the onion.

Or Stir in 200 g peeled and quartered tomatoes or 2 level tbsps. tomato paste when adding the stock.

Or After about 10 minutes' simmering, add 1 small pkt. frozen peas or prawns or 100–200 g leftover cooked meat or frankfurter sausages, cut into small pieces.

Or Pour a can of mushroom or tomato soup over the rice instead of stock.

Or Hard-boil 4 eggs, slice and chop them and add to the risotto just before serving.

Risotto—another traditional Italian dish—is ideal for a party, as it keeps hot for some time without spoiling. Either leave it in a pan with a close-fitting lid over a low heat or—a safer way—in a casserole covered with a lid or foil in a 150°C. (300°F.), mark 1 oven. Add some extra stock before serving, if it is rather dry.

STUFFED GREEN PEPPERS

Ingredients

4 green peppers
2 rashers of bacon, rinded
2 medium-sized onions
2–3 mushrooms
15 g lard
300 g minced beef
125 ml bouillon cube stock
Salt and pepper
1 level tbsp. flour
1 small can of tomato
  soup

Utensils

Chopping board
Knife, tablespoon, teaspoon,
  wooden spoon
2 saucepans
Plate
Measuring jug
Small basin
Ovenproof dish

1 Heat the oven to 190°C. (375°F.), mark 5.

2 Cut off the stalk end of the peppers, to form a " lid ", and remove all the pips from the inside, using a spoon (picture A).

3 Place the peppers in a pan of cold salted water, bring to the boil and boil for 5 minutes, remove from the water and drain well.

4 Chop the bacon, peel and chop the onions and wash and slice the mushrooms.

5 Melt the fat in the saucepan, fry the bacon until golden-brown, add the onions and mushrooms and fry until soft. Add the minced beef and fry until brown.

6 Add the stock, salt and pepper and cook for 10 minutes (picture B).

7 Mix the flour with a little cold water in a basin (picture C), add this to the meat mixture, stirring well, and simmer for 5 minutes.

8 Stand the green peppers upright in an ovenproof dish, fill with the meat mixture and put a " lid " back on each (picture D). Pour the tomato soup round them.

9 Cover with a lid or foil and bake in the centre of the oven for 30 minutes.

Note: Choose green peppers, as the red and yellow ones are apt to be hotter.

Putting a vegetable such as peppers or onions into cold salted water and bringing to the boil before cooking is known as " blanching " ; some people do it to prevent the flavour being too strong in the finished dish.

KEBABS

A kebab is made by threading an assortment of small pieces of food on a skewer and grilling. In the Near East, where kebabs originated, they were made up of lean cubes of lamb, pieces of onion and a few pieces of bay leaf ; pieces of tomato and green pepper are now included in many cases. In this country and in America, where kebabs are very popular, any of the following foods may be used: frankfurter sausages, luncheon meat, ham, bacon, kidney, liver, steak, lean lamb, apple and banana (dipped in lemon juice to prevent browning), pineapple, tomato, pepper and onion. Here are some typical kebab recipes, with quantities sufficient in each case to make 4 skewers:

BACON AND FRANKFURTER

Allow 8 small rashers of streaky bacon, 2 bananas, 2 frank-furters and 4 tomatoes.

Remove the rind from the bacon rashers; peel the banana and cut it into 4 pieces. Wrap each piece of banana in a rasher of bacon. Cut each frankfurter into 4 pieces and halve the tomatoes. Thread the pieces of frankfurter, the bacon-wrapped banana and the half-tomatoes alternately on to 4 long skewers. See below for method of cooking.

SAUSAGE-MEAT BALLS AND MUSHROOMS

Allow 200 g pork sausage-meat, 100 g mushrooms and 4 onions. Divide the sausage-meat into 12 portions and form each into a ball. If the mushrooms are large, cut into quarters. Cut the onions into quarters. Thread the sausage-meat balls, mushroom pieces and onion quarters alternately on to 4 long skewers.

LUNCHEON MEAT WITH PINEAPPLE

Allow 1 small can of luncheon meat, 4 small onions (or 1 large one cut in segments) and 1 small can of pineapple chunks.

Open the can of luncheon meat and cut the contents into 1 cm slices, then into 1 cm cubes. Peel the onions and cut in quarters. Open and drain the can of pineapple. Thread the cubes of meat, pieces of onion and pineapple alternately on 4 long skewers. (If preferred, you can substitute 4 small washed mushrooms for the pineapple.)

Cooking and Serving

Melt 50 g butter, brush the pieces of food with this and sprinkle well with salt and pepper. Heat the grill and place the skewers on the rack. Cook under a moderate heat for about 5 minutes, then turn the skewers over and cook for a further 5 minutes, or until the food is done. Kebabs can be served with boiled rice, mashed potatoes, crisps, salad or crisp French bread, or on their own, as a snack. They also make good food for parties and barbecues.

To make a Barbecue Sauce warm together in a saucepan 2 tbsps. Worcestershire sauce, 2 tbsps. tomato sauce, 1 level tsp. sugar, 2 tsps. vinegar, 15 g butter, a pinch of salt, a pinch of pepper, 3 tbsps. water and 1 small onion, finely chopped.

CURRY

Ingredients	Utensils
2 onions	Cook's knife, vegetable knife,
450 g stewing steak	wooden spoon, teaspoon
25 g margarine	Chopping board
1 level tbsp. curry	1 medium-sized saucepan
powder	with lid, 1 large saucepan
1 level tbsp. flour	Measuring jug
25 g desiccated coconut	Sieve
25 g sultanas	Lemon squeezer
250 ml bouillon cube stock	Serving dish
Salt	
150 g long-grain rice	
1 lemon	

1 Peel and chop the onions finely. Cut the meat into even-sized pieces, trimming off any unwanted fat.

2 Melt the margarine in the medium-sized saucepan, add the onions and fry for 5 minutes, or until golden. Add the meat, curry powder, flour, coconut and sultanas (picture A) and stir over a low heat for a further 5 minutes.

3 Add the stock gradually to the meat mixture, stirring all the time (picture B). Season with salt to taste, cover the pan with the lid and simmer for about $1\frac{1}{2}$–2 hours, or until the meat is tender.

4 About 30 minutes before the curry is due to be served, half-fill the large pan with water, bring it to the boil and add 1 level tsp. salt. Put the rice in the sieve and rinse under the cold water tap.

5 Add rice to boiling water (picture C) and boil fast for about 20 minutes, or until grains are just tender.

6 Drain the rice in the sieve, then rinse it with cold water, return it to the saucepan, cover with a lid and place over a low heat. Heat gently for about 5 minutes, until the rice is dry and hot, shaking the pan from time to time so that the grains do not stick (picture D).

7 To serve the curry, squeeze the juice from half the lemon and stir into the mixture; taste and adjust seasoning if necessary. Pour into serving dish and surround with rice. Cut remaining lemon in wedges and use to garnish.

Note: In India the curry and rice would be served in separate bowls, with accompaniments such as poppadums (a sort of crisp pancake), chutney and sliced fruits and vegetables.

HUNGARIAN GOULASH

Ingredients

450 g stewing steak
50 g flour; salt
2 onions, 1 green pepper
25 g lard
1 level tsp. paprika
375 ml bouillon cube stock
250 g tomatoes (*or* 2 tbsps.
  tomato paste)

Utensils

Vegetable knife, cook's knife,
  tablespoon, wooden spoon
Chopping board
Plate
Saucepan and lid
Serving dish

1 Trim the meat and cut into even-sized pieces. Mix half the flour with a good sprinkling of salt on a plate and roll the meat in this until well coated.

2 Skin onions, cut green pepper in half and remove the " core " and seeds (picture A): chop onion and pepper.

3 Melt lard in a saucepan and fry onion and green pepper for 5 minutes. Next add meat and paprika and fry for a further 5 minutes.

4 Stir in remaining flour, then stock. Peel and quarter tomatoes and add these or the tomato paste (picture B).

5 Cover pan and simmer gently for 1½–2 hours, or until meat is tender. Transfer to a hot serving dish. Dumplings or noodles are often served in a border round goulash.

Notes

1 Traditionally, goulash is cooked in 250 ml stock and 125 ml beer is added after 1 hour.

2 Continental cooks would use more paprika—at least 2 level tsps.—to give the correct red colour and hot flavour.

3 *Dumplings* to accompany the goulash can be made as follows: (i) Sift 150 g self-raising flour and ½ level tsp. salt into a mixing bowl; rub in 25 g margarine until the mixture looks like fine breadcrumbs, then stir in 1 level tsp. mixed herbs or caraway seeds. (ii) Add cold water a little at a time, stirring with a round-bladed knife, until a soft dough is formed. (iii) Cut into 12 pieces, then, using your floured hands, roll into balls. (iv) Bring a saucepan half-filled with water to the boil, drop in dumplings (picture C) and boil for about 25 minutes, or until tender. (v) Lift out carefully and serve with the gouiash (picture D).

4 *Noodles:* Cook 150 g in boiling salted water for 20 minutes, drain, add a knob of butter and mix well.

A
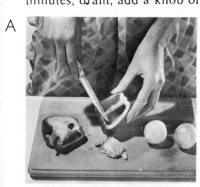

·B
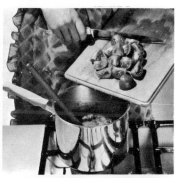

C

D

MENUS

FROM RECIPES TO MEALS

In this final section of the book are some simple menus. They are worked out mainly with dishes you have already made, to show you how these can be combined to provide meals for several different occasions. Apart from the snack meal on this page, the menus have been planned for you to carry out with a partner. When you have done this once, and got used to working to a plan, you will find you can begin to make your own menus, shopping lists and time-plans, using the other recipes given in this book.

AN EASY SNACK FOR YOURSELF

SCRAMBLED EGG WITH BACON
AN APPLE
A MILKY DRINK

Things you will need:
  1–2 rashers of bacon
  1 thick slice of bread
  Butter
  1 egg
  1 tbsp. milk
  Salt and pepper

An eating apple (or other fruit)
165 ml milk or milk and water
Instant coffee or chocolate powder
Sugar (optional)

Order of work

1 Trim the rind from the bacon and cut the rasher into small pieces.

2 Fry the bacon gently.